This is not intended as a children's book as such. The surprise is that all the events actually took place but Sue has enriched them by weaving fictional stories around her memories. The stories are of three children, Sue, her sister and brother, growing up in the 1960s and initially written as simple jottings for their Mum, Ann, from 2018 when she lived in a care home, because Ann would frequently say, "Do you remember, when you were little, you did so and so." She loved reading these stories.

Times have changed irrevocably since then. This collection of short stories is nostalgic for a way of life gone, but equally reveals some of the historical changes in the last 65 years.

The stories took on greater significance when Ann sadly passed away in 2024. They now honour the memory of Ann and her husband Andrew as well as keeping part of their family history alive.

Whether you want a good humorous read or are interested in the historical angle – this book is for you.

This book is published by

SUE LINES
PUBLISHING

First published in Great Britain as a softback original in 2025

ISBN. 978-1-9192091-0-4

Ann and Andrew, Never Forgotten

CONTENTS

Our Little World
1956–1967

Key

- A Our House
- B Our School
- C Our Bridges
- D Church / Canada Hall
- E Shoe Shop
- F Ladybird Shop
- G Post Office
- H Bon Bon Sweet Shop
- I Our Dentist
- J The Wreck
- K Lodge & Old Car
- L Watching Old Crocks

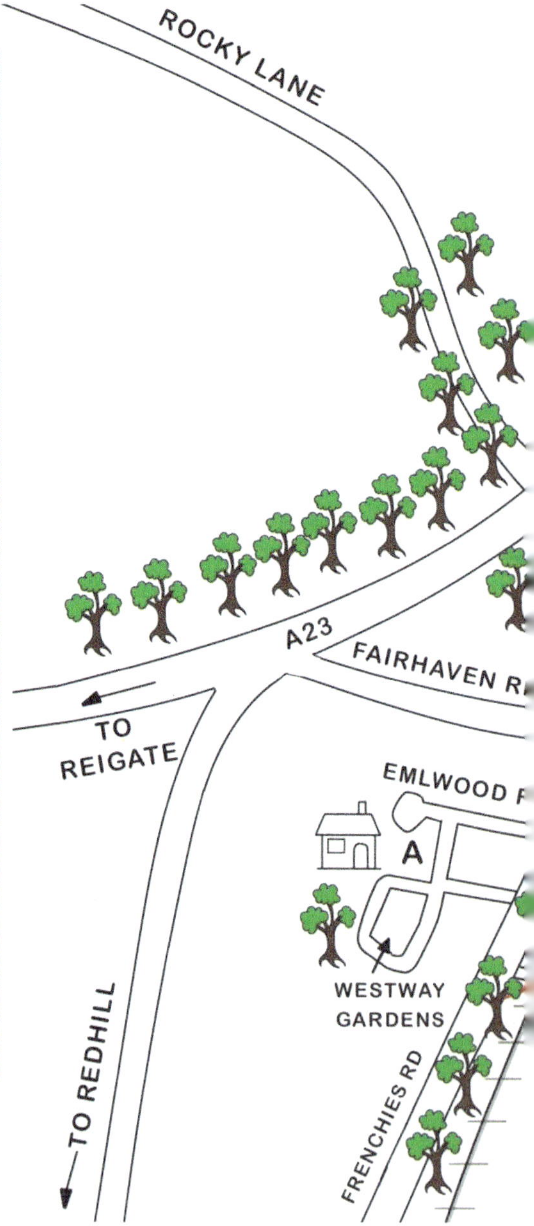

SCHOOL HILL
B
I
G
H
F
E
D
BATTLEBRIDGE LANE
NUTFIELD RD
TO BRIGHTON TRAIN
QUARRY LINE
RAILWAY SIDINGS
SAND QUARRY

1. It Happened in the Kitchen

A muffled "Click." Then all enveloping blackness. "Oh, not again," said a resigned voice as, yet again, the house was plunged into darkness. During the record freezing temperatures of the winter of 1955/56, with such heavy snowfall, most of Britain was paralysed, resulting in frequent power cuts. A massive electricity cut happened in January, just a few months after my Mum and Dad had moved into their brand new three- bedroom semi in Westway Gardens. This event took place a couple of months before I bounced into the world. Very early one morning Dad had gone off to work as usual although he had to struggle his way through the snowdrifts to the railway station. He left Mum with her mother, in the kitchen. This room had one door into our small hallway and another to the lounge and they were both closed. And the window curtains were also shut tight to keep out the cold air and draughts. The gloomy kitchen was lit by candles. Both adults were swathed in extra clothes and in Mums case, she was also wrapped in blankets. Granny had sat my heavily pregnant Mum in front of the open door of the kitchen gas oven – hot air escaping and pouring over Mum to keep her warm. Fortunately, in those days gas cookers didn't need electricity to spark them into action. There they would both sit huddled together, until at some point the electric light bulbs sprang into action again. And when Dad arrived home from work, he'd sort out our Parkray heater so hot water flowed through all the radiators to warm the whole house again until the next power cut. Needless to say, the sub-zero conditions played a significant part in my early arrival into this world.

* * * * *

Our kitchen became the heart of the home. Beyond this room was a coal bunker which opened out into the kitchen. In the late 1950s a fridge was still beyond the means of the average person. So, Dad, as ever resourceful, converted the space into a larder so food could be kept at a cooler temperature. When Mum was occupied in another room, I'd often struggle to wrench this door open – tiny fingers struggling to stretch upwards to reach the brass handle and push it open. When I had managed this feat I'd be rewarded by the sight and smells of endless shelves of delicacies; sparkly glass bottles stuffed full of pickled vegetables, yesterday's left-over meat covered in a lace doily, loaves of white bread, vegetables of all varieties and colours, a gleaming glass jug of homemade lemonade – murky with a rim of lemon pieces floating at the top, a row of tiny glass bottles containing food colourings – Mums favourite, so she had told me, was cochineal – a red colour, and the China butter container and the cheese carousel, a jelly sitting in its bunny rabbit tin mould, and best of all, the cake tins, which try as I often did, I could not reach as the tins had been placed on a shelf purposely beyond my reach.

* * * * *

Some years later, we did get a fridge. The big day arrived – the tradesmen wheeled it in from their van, heaving the heavy box up the entrance step and pushing it gently into the kitchen. They ripped the new cardboard packaging off to reveal a white metal box, plugged in the electric socket to the wall and then manoeuvred the hefty box into position. As they left the house one of the men called out, as if an afterthought, "It's all ready to use now." But we didn't rush to open the fridge door. Instead, we all stood, in rigid silence, eyes only focussed on the white metal box that had invaded our kitchen. We stared

FLOU

at the fridge, marvelling at its red top and gleaming appearance. Time somehow stopped as we children, and even Mum, continued to stand beside this new contraption. Every now and then Mum would stretch out her hand towards the fridge door, hesitate and then withdraw her arm to the comfort of her apron pocket. Even Mum was too scared to open the door, let alone put anything in it. When Dad came home from work that evening, I'm sure he had a grin on his face when he told our still anxious Mum, that she could put food in our new fridge.

* * * * *

As we grew older Mum let us help with cake making. We would squabble amongst ourselves as to who did what. "It's my turn," said Judy. I pushed her away from the table, and shouted "No it's not, it's mine." Mum intervened and marched one of us to the sink. She was strict about us washing our hands first, for more often than not minutes earlier we had been digging with our bare hands in the garden (especially when we decided that we could tunnel through to Australia by digging a hole in the soil - we kept on trying for days until another equally far-fetched idea grabbed our attention). Putting a chair up against the sink, Mum then beckoned us, one by one to clamber up and stand on the chair seat. She would turn the hot and cold taps on and scrub our dirty, brown hands and arms and our smeary faces with a huge block of soap. Next, a cotton apron, usually an old one of hers or Dads, was, she said, essential attire for real cooks. These aprons would dangle to near floor length on all three of us. Mum would then wrap the apron strings around our tiny waists twice or three times before tying them in a bow. "Who wants to make some ice-cream," said Mum as she looked at our beaming faces. "Me, me, me," we all shrieked in near- unison. We stood around the oblong kitchen table, usually it was covered in a PVC tablecloth. One of us volunteered to clean the surface – we'd delight at hearing the squeaks as the wet cloth was rubbed over it. A large ceramic bowl appeared and Mum mixed extra-sweetened condensed milk with jelly in it. We all took turns to stir the metal spoon around and around till Mum used an old-fashioned hand whisk to froth up the creamy liquid. She looked at Judy as she poured the mixture into a metal container and said "can you open the fridge door please?" Switching her gaze to me saying "And Susan, can you open the ice compartment," - Mum slid in the container onto the tiny shelf and sighed in relief that we children were at last behaving obediently.

Another day we helped to make fairy cakes. Out came the ceramic bowl to which Mum placed all the ingredients we'd helped find from the cupboards, the fridge and the larder. Most times we'd happily take turns to stir the smooth mounds of sugary mixture around the bowl as well as spooning dollops into feather-like patterned paper-cases. Mock fist- fighting and painful elbow nudging between the three of us resulted in the winner getting to lick the bowl; to taste the sweetness of the remaining traces of creamy smears was the highlight of all baking sessions. Much to Mums exasperation our greedy tongues ventured into the depths of the bowl resulting in blobs of cake mixture covering our faces and hair. Later, Mum would ice the cakes and then it was our job to sprinkle hundreds and thousands over the icing, although most landed on the tablecloth then dribbled onto the floor.

* * * * *

Every Easter, at breakfast time, we'd hear the sound of eggs being dropped into pans of boiling water on the gas stove. That year us children had sat, for once, patiently at the kitchen table watching Mum do the dangerous stuff. The eggshells were white and Mum had poured a few drops of food colouring into each pan. The cooked eggs were then put in a Pyrex bowl in front of us on the table. At this point our patience evaporated as three sets of tiny arms collided in the bowl to fight over the choice of coloured eggs. "I want the yellow one, cos I'm older than you," I shouted at Judy. She snatched the yellow egg out of my hand yelling, "No, it's mine, you have the pink one." "Girls, girls," said Mum with a slight look of irritation on her face, "Please calm down, this year Judy can have the yellow one and next year," she looked directly at me, "Susan can." Judy and I sneered at each other while we ate our boiled eggs and soldiers, occasionally (when Mum wasn't looking) we'd punch each other's arms. Stephen, glancing at his sister's bad behaviour, quietly munched his way through his blue boiled egg. Later that morning, the boiled egg spat long forgotten, and Mum was in the garden, I sneaked up to the larder and managed to yank open the door.

My little eyes scanned each shelf – I knew what I was looking for – Easter teeth bashers, as we children called them. I looked again, up and down the shelves until a brightly coloured bag caught my attention. Yes, that was it. I stretched out my arm up to the shelf, then stood on tip-toes but couldn't quite reach the bag. "Susan," bellowed Mum, who was by then standing right behind me, "What are you doing?" She pulled me out of the larder and closed the door, loudly clicking the latch shut. I hung my head down and mumbled, "The little Easter eggs, the small chocolate ones covered in white sugary icing.

Our favourite," I added as I continued looking at the floor. Mum put her arm round my shoulder. "Next time," she said softly, "Don't go slinking into the larder on your own – ask me first." I held my head up and sighed and walked sluggishly towards the lounge. I then heard the sound of the larder latch unclick, turning my head, I saw Mum as she followed me in to the lounge carrying the bag of teeth bashers.

* * * * *

We had a special picture hanging on one of the kitchen walls. Special because, as our family moved from house to house, that picture was always placed in each new kitchen. Just an ordinary cheap print – probably also in many other households too, but capable of transporting anyone (young or old) into a dream world of endless sunshine and relaxation. Within the bare wooden frame and under the glass lay a scene of a sleepy and content Mediterranean village, with a vibrant blue cloudless sky, whitewashed buildings, and a serene female figure (a slight passing resemblance to Mum I thought), her dress catching the intense rays of the sun. This scene was quite a contrast to the realities of our chaotic kitchen and our lives.

* * * * *

CHANDOS

Apart from cooking, the kitchen was also the laundry room. No matter what, a Monday was always the laundry day. We had a great big metal washing machine where clothes and other laundry was stuffed into a round hole on the top of the machine and then a thin metal lid was placed over it and a big red button pressed to start the "swish swash" of the washing process. Once the machine had gurgled to a stop, the washing was clean, but dripping wet. We all helped to pull out a mangle from a store cupboard, and beneath this, a large metal bowl was located – expertly placed by Mum to catch all the water drips. Sometimes I would help Mum by turning the mangle handle as she fed the water- soaked laundry, one piece at a time, through the two rollers to squeeze the water out. Occasionally, and without thinking, I'd knock the bowl from its position as my body and little feet edged closer to the mangle causing pools of water to cascade onto the lino floor and onto my shoes and socks. The next stage was drying the washing. I can remember looking up at the ceiling as Mum pulled a rope to lower our laundry pulley to waist- height. Most households had one of these ceiling pulleys. The device, made by Dad I think, consisted of five or six long laths of wood threaded through two pieces of cast iron to anchor them into place. The cast iron 'anchors' resembled coat hangers in shape. But we children were more interested in the rope pulley system. When Mum wasn't around and there was no washing hanging on the slats, we'd heave the rope down, let go and this would send the whole contraption flying up to the ceiling resulting in an almighty "bang" as it hit the ceiling. Of course, we would then run away when it came crashing down. Sheets and larger items Mum pegged out to dry on one of the two clotheslines in the garden. One winters day the laundry literally froze and became solid; the wooden clothes-pegs iced up and where immoveable. Despite a strong breeze the sheets remained rigid.

Whilst Mum did most of the cooking we were regularly told to keep out of her way in the kitchen, especially when she was busy around the gas cooker. Standing near the connecting doorway between the lounge and kitchen I'd hear the sound of crockery being taken out of the cupboards, the metallic ringing of saucepans being put on the stove and the "plop plop" of prepared ingredients added. When steam ceased to emanate into our 'playroom', the lounge, we knew that tea was nearly ready. Without being asked Judy and I would mooch into the kitchen, chair legs scrapping across the floor as we scrambled onto our chairs to sit expectantly around the kitchen table. When Judy was a baby, she'd be looked after first – she was carefully put into her high-chair by Mum, and then given a rusk to chew on while I had to wait for what seemed like an eternity for my food to appear. Often, my beady eyes were looking round the kitchen as I contemplated the unfairness of the situation.

Chips had always been my favourite; there was no mistaking the sound of the oil in the chip pan bubbling and then sizzling as the basket of raw, sliced potatoes was lowered into the pan. And the smell of freshly cooked chips (topped off with lashings of tomato ketchup), made my mouth salivate with anticipation. This glorious event happened every Friday and with fish fingers, and on special occasions just chips.

Although one day this heavenly event was interrupted when the chip pan caught fire. The fire brigade was called to put out the blaze but we only got to see the aftermath – a black, charred chip pan barely distinguishable from the other pots and pans on the burnt stove, and the wall above was various shades of brown and black. Although the smoke had disappeared through the open windows a nauseating smell hovered and seeped into the rest of the house. We had bread and butter for tea that day, and not at the kitchen table.

Susan looking around kitchen wondering where her food is.

2 Mishaps in our Childhood

"Bang, bang, bang, bang." The noise was unmistakable and was coming from upstairs. Again, the bangs sounded even louder as Mum rushed up the stairs, two at a time, and I followed to see what all the commotion was about. My little sister, Judy, a mischievous toddler, could now be heard screaming at the top of her voice. "Mummy, Mummy," sobbed the little voice behind the bathroom door. Her little hands were beating on the wooden door as she shouted and sobbed. Mum tried to open the bathroom door by pushing the handle until her knuckles were white. "But I told you not to lock the bathroom door," she said to the closed door. More moans and wails and then sniffling from Judy. "See the little metal lock by the door handle – just slide it to the right," said my exasperated and yet concerned Mum. A moments silence, we both held our breathe, and then; bang, bang, bang. And more wails. "Just try," said Mum again, sweat marks were by now dribbling down her face, patiently adding "Put your hand up to the lock and slide it across." Piercing screams erupted, and more bangs. Turning to me, "Stay here Susan, I'm going to get your father," said Mum. I stood in silence, eyes pinned on the door handle, occasionally hearing muffled sobs from the other side of the door. Now and then the door-handle flickered, and the sobs would resume.

A while later Dad, who'd been at a neighbour's house, came bounding up the stairs and ran to the end of the narrow landing, closely followed by our neighbour – a big, stocky man. I retreated into my bedroom – it was inches away from the bathroom. Our tiny landing was by now crowded with three adults standing in-front of the locked door. Judy's screams had subsided, although the sound of sniffles could still be heard through the flimsy wooden door. "Judy," he said calmly, "It's Dad – can you hear me?" A pause, "Yes," Judy said, her voice barely audible. "Now Judy" said Dad, "I want you to get as far away from the door as you can as we are going to push the door in." Our neighbour and Dad put the palms of their hands against the door and pushed, and pushed. Eventually the wood started to rip and then the hinges on one side and the lock from the other gave way. The two pairs of hands swiftly caught the door as it fell into the bathroom. The adults hurtled in. I tried to peer into bathroom through the tangle of legs, trousers and Mums skirt. Underneath the basin I could see a shape of twisted cotton dungarees; Judy was curled up like a ball, her little arms and hands wrapped around her head, and she was whimpering. Mum rushed towards her, wrapping her loving arms around the toddler. I don't recall her ever locking that door again.

* * * * *

Family holidays were always an adventure. Since Mum passed her driving test and our parents got a car, we headed off every summer to 'somewhere in the west of the country'. Our second-hand (or 3rd or 4th hand) navy-blue Anglia, 649 BLM, complete with huge roof-rack, was loaded up with cases, rugs, picnic hamper, Calor-gas stove and other paraphernalia – leaving very little space for us five to squeeze into. The car trundled along the A25, a meandering, leafy, green edged road taking us west. Every year we'd pass through a tiny village (Abinger Hammer); "Arr..binge..eer Aam..mer, Arr..binge..er Ham..mer", us youngsters would sing as we passed under the clocktower with a figure of a metal man holding a hammer in his hand. And, like clockwork, every year Dad would explain to us that the metal man represented a blacksmith from a nearby forge. Sometimes, if we drove past dead on the hour, we'd get to see the metal man swinging his hammer and striking the bell hanging above him.

Minutes later, us three youngsters were still sitting happily in the back seat of the car singing 'Ar..binger Aaa..mmer, Arr..binge..eer..Aaammer', Mum turned the car onto another road. The grey asphalt road stretched out in front of the car, bending occasionally before disappearing into the hazy blue horizon. Lush green rolling meadows either side framed the shimmering heat of the road. Without warning, our smooth ride suddenly transformed into a bumping sensation from beneath us. Up down, up down – our bottoms jolting upwards towards the car roof and then falling back down onto the soft seats; the Anglia repeatedly juddered, as if crying out in pain, and weaved one way and then the other. Mum had long since put her foot down on the brakes. Our little Anglia slowly mounted the left-hand kerb of the road and came to an undignified stop in the long blades of springy grass. Of course, other motorists stopped to help. A broken axle was mentioned. A man in white overalls appeared. He disappeared under the open car bonnet and quite soon his overalls and bare-arms were stained with black engine oil. Within the hour our poor little broken-down car was repaired and the tiny blue Anglia with all its inhabitants continued westwards on the sparkling tarmac road.

* * * * *

Toddler, Stephen, would sit astride his baby rocker, face beaming and chuckling to himself as he bent forward and back rocking on the toy for hours. Known affectionately as his 'swanny rocker', the toy had at first been mine, then handed down to baby Judy, and finally passed down to baby Stephen. Mum would carry the metal swanny rocker to the kitchen or lounge for him; mainly to keep an eye on her mischievous child. After a few months, his chubby little legs and midriff had grown so much – he was too big for the swanny rocker. That springtime, Mum and Dad bought him a brand-new rocking horse. At first, the rocking horse was kept in the lounge, and then on warmer days, in the garden.

One Saturday Mum and Dad heaved the wooden rocking horse up the narrow stairs to his bedroom, placing it on the bare floor boards away from his bed and soft woven rug. Stephen would climb up onto the miniature horse, almost trapping his voluminous dungarees in the stirrups as he swung one leg over the horse; his bottom resting on the padded saddle. Clasping his stubby fingers around the handlebars, he plunged his tiny feet into the stirrups, lean forward so his chin touched the fluffy white mane, and roll his head and torso backwards. Sounds would reverberate around the house as the wooden rocker squeaked on the floor boards. Mealtimes were often temporarily halted when he shouted a gruff "No," to Mums request that he come down the stairs.

One weekend he shut his bedroom door and climbed on the white horse. Judy and I were playing in the room below. "Squeak, squeak," We could hear the sound clearly as the sound echoed around the room - on and on and on. But, after a while the squeaks turned to thumps.

Stephen – first time on new rocking horse.

Then the thumps turned to bangs and ear-piercing shrieks. Loud, urgent, footsteps disappeared up the stairs. Judy and I stood at the foot of the stairs, shifting from one foot to the other whilst peering up at our parents. “Follow me you two,” Dad shouted as he sprinted back down the stairs and past us. We followed and watched him yank and unhook a sturdy ladder from the garage wall; leaving a trail of cobwebs and a couple of long-haired spiders tottering down the wall of grey breeze blocks. A deep shiver ran through my body. Chilly arms bumped against each other as we both scampered outside into the warm comforting sunshine to see Dad now standing at the foot of the upright ladder. “Susan, Judy, stand each side of the ladder and hold tight so the ladder doesn’t move.” Our tense fingers gripped the metal ladder – we looked up as Dad climbed the rungs until he reached the open window of Stephens bedroom. He manoeuvred his lanky body through the window and vanished. Stephen, we found out later, had rocked his rocking horse so hard that it had glided across the floorboards. One of the handles on the rocking-horse then got wedged beneath the door-handle and stuck fast. After his rescue, his white horse was mainly confined to the lounge and on sunny days, to the garden.

* * * * *

“Sadie,” I shouted as I lunged across the carpet, failing once again to grab the tiny shape as it disappeared behind the sofa. Moments later, a furry honey-coloured object emerged from behind one of the sofa legs. This time Judy hurled herself towards the floor, missing the creature by inches. Sadie was our hamster and as a special treat Mum had let us bring her cage in the lounge. We had been watching Sadie play inside her wheel; her tiny body stretched out, small white paws constantly bounding up and down on the metal rungs of the treadmill and yet her body not going anywhere. Such was her determination - her bright eyes and long nose craning upwards as she focused on climbing up the inside of the wheel. Mesmerized by the spectacle, one of us reached into her cage and gently lifted her out. We took it in turns to stroke the bundle of soft feathery fur. It was my turn, I held her tightly in my hands, feeling her tiny heart racing against my cupped palms and then, almost recoiling, as her sharp nails punctured my skin. I felt sorry for the little creature; she must have been terrified. My hands reached down to floor level - I intended to let Sadie go back to the sanctuary of her cage. At the same moment, Mum came back from the garden and walked through the lounge door. "Susan, what are you doing" shouted Mum to me. Sadie leapt out of my now loosened fingers, jumped to the floor and ran.

"I told you three not to let her out of her cage," yelled Mum, while Sadie's head popped out from the back of the sofa. "And don't think I won't tell your father, because I will," she said sternly. Chaos reigned for the next few minutes; Mum darting this way and that, Judy and I sliding around the carpet and toddler Stephen shrieking with excitement as he jumped up and down at one end of the room. Sadie kept appearing at floor level from every piece of furniture in the room and then scampered off to hide somewhere else. Each time her little snout and beady eyes appeared, one of us would hurtle towards her, Judy or I usually crashing into a bookcase or the coffee table. Sadie was caught, eventually. Mum, her face flushed and lined with sweat, sighed with relief. She calmly locked Sadie's cage and took it back to the table in the lean-to at the back of the house. Returning to the lounge, her pursed lips and staring eyes lingered on us three children. "Well, you won't do that again," her eyes now bright as she grinned at us.

"Can you look behind that toy chest again," said a rather worn-out Mum as she tugged her sweaty strands of hair away from her face. "And you're sure you searched properly under your beds," she said whilst holding up an eiderdown which hung down from my bed. "Yes", I shouted, "Everywhere in this room, three times." I kicked the red painted toy chest – leaving reddish scuff marks on the toe of my new white shoe. Judy sat on her bed, arms folded and head bowed. She looked up as Mum said, "Downstairs children, time we started asking the neighbours. I'm sure someone is feeding him. Maybe he just wanted a change of scenery."

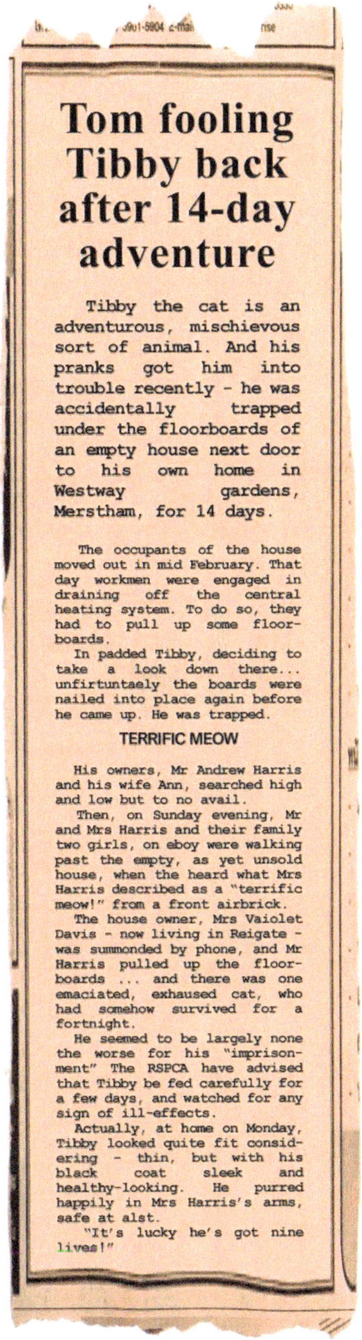

Tom fooling Tibby back after 14-day adventure

Tibby the cat is an adventurous, mischievous sort of animal. And his pranks got him into trouble recently - he was accidentally trapped under the floorboards of an empty house next door to his own home in Westway gardens, Merstham, for 14 days.

The occupants of the house moved out in mid February. That day workmen were engaged in draining off the central heating system. To do so, they had to pull up some floor-boards.

In padded Tibby, deciding to take a look down there... unfirtuntaely the boards were nailed into place again before he came up. He was trapped.

TERRIFIC MEOW

His owners, Mr Andrew Harris and his wife Ann, searched high and low but to no avail.

Then, on Sunday evening, Mr and Mrs Harris and their family two girls, on eboy were walking past the empty, as yet unsold house, when the heard what Mrs Harris described as a "terrific meow!" from a front airbrick.

The house owner, Mrs Vaiolet Davis - now living in Reigate - was summonded by phone, and Mr Harris pulled up the floor-boards ... and there was one emaciated, exhaused cat, who had somehow survived for a fortnight.

He seemed to be largely none the worse for his "imprison-ment" The RSPCA have advised that Tibby be fed carefully for a few days, and watched for any sign of ill-effects.

Actually, at home on Monday, Tibby looked quite fit consid-ering - thin, but with his black coat sleek and healthy-looking. He purred happily in Mrs Harris's arms, safe at alst.

"It's lucky he's got nine lives!"

Tibby hadn't come home for three days. He was our cat, although Mum and Dad fed him, and 'dealt' with his litter tray – a container filled with a revolting mixture of powdery ash and smelly cat wee. But we loved him (except when he was squatting in his tray). Days passed, no Tibby. Each day we would run around the garden shouting 'Tibby, Tibby', until our hoarse voices admitted defeat. Sometimes we'd mooch around the house in silence, shoulders arched, little feet dragging along the floor. Mum must have enjoyed this contrast from normality; we children were no longer running hither and thither; voices shrill with excitement. At the end of the second week, we had all but given up on seeing Tibby again. On this day, we were walking back from school in what had become our unusual silence, we trundled slowly along the pavement, with Mum holding 4-year-old Stephen's hand tightly. We approached the corner of our quiet crescent, and began to turn right. All the gardens had open boundaries to the pavement; no fences or bushes, just grass and a few multi-coloured flower beds in some gardens. Suddenly, an audible "Ssssss, sssssss," caught our attention. We all looked around us, but couldn't see anything. "Sssss, meow, meowwwwww," the noise intensified. "It's a cat," exclaimed Mum, her eyes darting between the gardens until she had located where the sound was coming from. Dropping Stephen's hand, she ran into the corner house front garden and stopped by the brick wall of the house. Crouching down by an air- brick she peered through the holes. "Oh Tibby, Tibby, it's you," she cried.

Two weeks before this, the Davidson family had moved out and the house was still empty. During the removals some of the floorboards were removed and later sealed down. Between these two events Tibby managed to get himself trapped beneath the wooden boards. When the story of Tibby's mishap was reported in the local paper, Dad carefully cut out the article for us. We took it in turns to show and tell our friends how our cat Tibby had suddenly become famous due to his unfortunate antics!

* * * * *

"You can't catch me," shrieked Stephen as Judy as I raced along the station platform trying to catch him, leaving a haze of gritty dust behind us. That hot summer we were staying right in the heart of the New Forest – in a converted railway carriage, in a siding. Dads' teenage cousin had joined us too. Dad's railway enthusiasm had rubbed off to us youngsters, we enjoyed the experience of rural station life; watching the clunk of the wooden red and white semaphore signals as they dropped down or flew up, peering into the dark ticket-office watching for any signs of life, standing high up in the middle of the footbridge; waving our tiny arms and cheering as a train swooshed beneath us. The station wasn't busy, so we could safely play on both platforms, although only when Dad gave us permission. Occasionally he'd yell at us, "Stusan, Stuussan, come back here," provoking giggles from us all as he always got our names muddled up whenever he was angry with us.

"Eeny, meeny, minny, moe," said Stephen, pointing his little fingers at Judy, "You're 'it'." Judy sprang round, ran off up the footbridge and disappeared onto the other platform. I charged up the steps, my pint- sized legs could just about manage two steps at a time, until I felt my side ache. Stopping on the high walkway, my chest swelled as I took in air. My t-shirt and shorts were wet with sweat. I stood on tiptoes to look over the bridge balustrade and spun my eyes along the opposite platform – "I can see you," I whispered to myself. A shifting shadow was visible behind the whitewashed waiting room. Exploding with energy my body hurtled down the opposite steps, knees bending, shoulders arched, I jumped high into the air to bypass the remaining four steps.

Susan holding her poorly knee as she is sitting beside railway camping coach.

But, only one foot landed on the gritty surface, my right knee thumped to the ground and slid along the gravel. “Stuuusan,” hollered my dad with a mixture of concern and anger. An hour later a local pharmacist tweezered out most of the black grit from my potholed red knee. Smelling strongly of antiseptic and swathed with flimsy lint bandages around my knee joint, I hopped along the pavement, but clinging tightly on to my Mums arm. We didn’t play tag again that summer.

* * * * *

3 The Treehouse

In the early years of living at our house in Westway Gardens we had no garden. Well, a brown muddy patch of pitted earth, left by the house- builders, including a line of trees, with the expectation that the new residents would create their own garden. Over time Mum and Dad set to, although it must have been sometime after I was born in 1956, a few months after they moved in, or even after my sister and brother were born. Gardening was probably the last thing on my parent's minds as they juggled with the demands of bringing up three young energetic children, jobs and all the other normal day to day activities thrust upon them. Alas, this was the age when all mod cons were only just beginning to appear, and being young my parents had few of these labour-saving devices.

The row of trees at the end of the garden was well established and grew fast. These ten-to fifteen-foot-high trees formed a swaying green boundary, in between our back garden and that of the back gardens of part of Elmwood Road which runs parallel to our house in Westway Gardens. There were no woods in the vicinity just this orderly line of oak and elm trees separating the gardens in each road. During winter months, when there were no leaves on the trees, we could easily see into the back garden of the house backing onto our home. "Look, look," I exclaimed one weekend to Judy, my voice was high-pitched with excitement. Judy and I jumped up and down, laughing and singing as we both called out to our parents. "What's all the fuss about?", said Dad as he emerged from the garage. Mum then stepped out of the kitchen with a perplexed look on her face. Judy and I, still bouncing up and down, pointed to two tiny figures playing in the garden behind our garden. One was obviously a girl, her long-sleeved dress ballooning in the strong breeze, whilst the other, a boy, was wearing shorts, a jersey and a pair of black wellington boots. He appeared to be spinning around with a stick in his hand – maybe it was a model airplane? "Mum, Dad, they look like the same ages as us; can we go and play with them?", we shrieked in crescendo. I began to pull back the narrower tree branches to see if there was a way through to the other garden. As I stepped through the narrow arch-way I'd created Dad grabbed me by my duffle coat. "Susan, Susan, you can't do that", he bellowed as he dragged me backwards by my coat sleeves into our garden. "Please, please," I persisted. Mum was holding Judy's hand although Judy kept trying to make a dash for the little arch-way. Both our voices and bright eyes were glowing with excitement as we implored our parents over and over again. But, as usual Mum intervened saying those magic words, "It's teatime," and immediately our attention switched. Fish fingers, peas, powdered potato Smash and lashings of tomato ketchup got in the way of our plans. And during the next few days there were heavy snowfalls and countless other distractions so we didn't get to meet our little neighbours till the following Spring.

* * * * *

In our garden one particular oak tree stood out from the other trees. Its leaves shimmered in the breeze and the old gnarled branches appeared mysteriously to beckon us – our fascination began. We, or more likely Dad, noticed that its chunky trunk and plethora of branches were ideally suited to building a treehouse within the sturdy boughs.

Mum standing beside treehouse with Susan and Judy standing on newly constructed treehouse platform.

Dad was a draughtsman and an engineer, so he was used to constructing all sorts of things. He was also inventive and over the next few years built, we thought, the most splendid treehouse that us three youngsters had ever seen. A true treehouse, constructed from newly hewn planks of wood, each one precisely and lovingly placed and hammered together and filling the air with a pungent aroma. This treehouse didn't have brightly painted walls or a roof, but was simplicity in design and function. Although, in later years, each summertime Dad made us a roof-covering for the treehouse – a thick striped canvas awning tied to the higher tree branches. We'd stand on the wooden platform stretching our arms up to feel and then smell the musty canvas. Over time, Dad constructed more horizontal platforms to our treehouse, each higher than the main area. These platforms, all carefully nailed into place, straddled right across the thick branches. Dad had created a special space – to us little ones he was a professional treehouse maker. He had made us a castle in the sky.

Dad also made and hung a simple rope and slat ladder securely from the first platform of our treehouse. The frayed ends of the rope would flop down to the base of our tree, mixing happily with the dusty soil – until small feet began climbing the ladder and the rope ends were suddenly whisked into the air. As time passed, the little patch of dry soil spread out from beneath the treehouse, the more we used the ladder, the more it spread. Needless to say, on days when we had heavy rain the whole area would resemble a giant-sized rock cake covered in black treacle. After a particular deluge of rain, the indentations in the rock cake increased. Swish, swash, squel…ccch – we children loved to hear the sucking noises made by our wellington boots as we walked through the mud. As well as stepping into the puddles all around the tree. Squelch, splash,

ZapSpla....ttt - all the rain water would be sprayed everywhere leaving trails of muddy water all over us. Our clothes and hair were caked with brown slimy mud. Bathtime that day was filled with several very serious telling offs from Mum. From that day on even us brazen youngsters would not venture anywhere near the end of our garden when we had heavy rain; fearful because of the telling off we'd get from Mum and Dad.

* * * * *

"You can't touch us," we'd often shriek to Dad as he stood beneath the tree looking up at us. Our little legs jangling hither and thither above the reach of his outstretched arms. He'd then stand on his toes, pretending to groan and then laughing whilst saying, "Oh, oh, I'm nearly there, I've nearly got your toes," until he fell back on the grass huffing and puffing to admit defeat. We children would frequently pull up the rope ladder to stop undesirables from invading our treehouse. And Dads 6-foot body, even with his arms outstretched above him and standing on his toes, could not touch our feet. The treehouse was our castle and parents were not allowed to join us!

The treehouse became our special fortress. One by one we'd all clamber up the rickety rope ladder onto the sturdy plinths of wood, stand up and survey the territory; our garden, our house, the neighbours' houses and beyond to the distant rooftops and the blobs of greenery here and there. We would yell at the top of our voices, probably to Mum, as she watched us through the open kitchen window, "I'm the king of the castle, get down you dirty rascal." Giggles and laughter emanated from deep within the leaf filled boughs. A few moments later we'd repeat the ditty, but in hushed voices, "I'm the king of the castle and I can climb even higher than you." Each child daring the other to crawl further along the branches. We were young, lithe and had no fear. Heaving and twisting our hot bodies just a little bit further along the ribbed boughs, we'd often scrape our flesh on the jagged bark, but we'd never fall to the ground. Mum, but certainly not Granny, usually told us off at bath-time when they saw the bruises and splintered skin on our battered bodies. Immediately Mum would be met by defiant stares from six little unblinking eyes, followed by smirky grins, giggles and much splashing of the by now brown bath-water.

Granny supervising bathtime for the three children.

* * * * *

One day, my Granny, Mums Mum, gave me an old-fashioned silver object to keep. I treasured it, constantly rolling it around in my hand to explore the nooks and crannies of the blemished and time-dented piece of silver. It was special, like a lock of hair in a locket. One summer day, after playing with it, I thrust it into the back pocket of my shorts and within minutes had forgotten all about it. Hours later I played in the treehouse. “Teas ready”, Mum called from the kitchen. Her voice was muffled as by now we had a lean-to in front of the kitchen, so it was harder to hear anyone calling out to us from within the house. I scrambled down the ladder first. Judy and Stephen carried on playing above me. Seconds later I felt something flutter onto my hair, and then all over my head. Realizing that my brother and sister had sprinkled leaves on my head, I moved away from the tree and shook my head and body so violently that the leaves scattered all around me. Suddenly gripped with panic, cold goosebumps appeared on my arms. I dipped my hand into an .... empty pocket, “Where is it?” I said to myself. My sister and brother pushed past me and ran to the kitchen. I re-climbed the ladder, scrabbled through many of the leaves and branches, I looked on ledges, I pulled back leaves – hands darting here and there. In desperation I half fell back down the rope ladder and began sifting through the dry soil at the base of the tree. Mum called again with a sternness that had to be obeyed, “Susan, your teas ready.” I trudged hopelessly into the house, head down. During the coming days and
weeks, I searched endlessly for the object. I didn’t tell anyone and I never found it.

* * * * *

Before long we invited our friends to join us in our castle. Very soon, our treehouse was the envy of all our friends

Susan, Judy, Stephen and friends standing in treehouse.

– a private space where adults were not allowed. Of course, our little neighbours from the garden behind ours were our first friends to venture up into our treehouse. The little girl was roughly the same age as me and the small boy was a bit younger than Judy. Within the next few months many of the other children from our road also joined us. As our treehouse gained in popularity, children from further afield such as our school friends in the nearby village of Merstham and from other parts of Redhill were invited too.

And then we met a new friend who lived even further away – in France! In the 1960's it was commonplace for French students to stay with British families and study here during the school holidays. Each participating family was paid a fee for the French child's bed and board. Our tiny three-bedroom house could only just squeeze in our family: Mum, Dad and us three growing youngsters. Somehow a camp bed was jammed into the area between my sisters' bed and mine; often resulting in a tangle of sheets and blankets fighting for the space. For several years running, Francoise would arrive in the summer sunshine and depart six-weeks later as our long school holidays were drawing to a close. Francoise was a year or two older than me. She too loved our treehouse, mainly because she had no garden - her family lived in an apartment building in the dense claustrophobic streets of Paris. Shrieks, laughter and French voices often travelled through the branches when Francoise stayed. All three of us children would mimic her French accent as she attempted to speak in English. "Zee laider," we would say as she approached the rope ladder to the treehouse. "Ah, oui," she'd say as she began climbing up the rungs – hands gripping the thick rope, one foot at a time, "un deux trois".

Laughing and giggling we children attempted to repeat her words: “Wee, une duu twaa.” When we were called into the kitchen for tea we would shout out “Ooo, lar teehuss. Wee, wee, wee,” and other such words. If Mum heard the sound of our ridiculous voices, we all knew we were in for a telling off. But, sniggering and giggling we brushed off her stern words. The moment our tea arrived on the kitchen table the treehouse was forgotten. And when a few years later we moved to a new home, a Victorian terrace house – with no trees in the garden, the treehouse soon became a distant memory.

* * * * *

4 Santa

We children stood huddled around the loft ladder as Dad climbed down the metal steps. A layer of dust had arrived at our nostrils before he stood on the carpet – provoking twitching, scratching and eventually sneezes from us all. The box he carried was no ordinary box; it had a special smell and that smell heralded the start of Christmas. We followed him into the lounge as he carried the box; the brown cardboard was slightly sagging at the corners through overuse. The lid was lifted – a musty unique smell evaporated into the room and we all peered into an organized tangle of coloured tissue papered objects; green, red and some blue. Each year this event was repeated and each year we knew that Christmas had arrived when the musty boxes appeared. Although our tree had been chosen – roots as well, brought home, planted in a bucket and manoeuvred into a corner of the living room – it never felt like Christmas until our noses smelt last year's fragrances lingering in that box.

Dad would always fix the fairy lights around the tree. And on most occasions, we'd look expectantly at the tree, hoping to see it all lit-up when Dad turned on the socket – usually, nothing would happen. He'd then have to take out and check each bulb while we children giggled for some minutes at this customary hold-up. "Take it in turns children," Mum or Dad would say as we turned to the boxes. We'd immediately obey as we remembered from the year before how delicate this treasure was. Gently picking up one of the objects, I unravelled the tissue paper. The crinkled paper was soft, almost like fabric, used so many times – I fingered the crumples and thought they were about to fall apart. Inside the soft wrapping I lifted out a silver bauble, holding the wire clip as I dangled it in the air. Each bauble was made of wafer-thin glass and coated with metallic paint; red, green, silver, gold, and a few turquoise and lavender colours too. Some were round in shape, others shaped like a pendant, and a few had a scattering of white encrustations on top of the paint to resemble snow. Soon all the baubles, wooden Santa's and other toy objects hung around the tree – year after year, as we grew taller, the less Mum and Dad had to help. Next, from another box we pulled out strands of silver tinsel and ribbons of cotton wool snow; both draped generously around and between the baubles and fairy lights. Finally, after several hands sifted through masses of crepe paper, the fairy was found; complete with stiff white net wings and long flowing dress, one hand holding a silver wand and star, and silky knickers. Her white dress was grey in places, her wings had seen better days and one point was missing from the star. Nevertheless, we children always squabbled as to who got to put her on top of the tree. One of us would be scooped up by six-foot high Dad, held carefully in his arms, one of the child's arms clinging to his shirt while the other arm stretched out to reach the top of the tree. Mum would then lean on tiptoe to help us drop the fairy onto the tallest sprig on the pine tree.

* * * * *

"Wake up, wake up", I whispered loudly to Judy, tugging at the blankets on her bed. Judy's head emerged from her sleep-filled cocoon. It was still dark, although some light was now beginning to shine around the edge of the window curtains. Sitting bolt upright, she asked, "Did we miss Santa?" I was holding my stocking – in the half-light I could see and feel the bulges that were crammed full of gifts. At the end of her bed, I found hers too. Handing it to Judy I said "Yes, I don't know how, cos we were both awake most of the night. I didn't hear a thing." "Neither did I," she replied. Adding, "Perhaps Santa puts a spell on people so they can't hear or see him? And the presents appear by magic." I hit the bed- clothes in annoyance, saying "I promise next year I'll stay awake all night." "So will I," she said while she tipped the contents of the stocking all around her. I drew back one curtain – the soft morning light still contained shadows, but they were ebbing away rapidly.

Each red stocking was a real sock; long stretchy wool knitted in ribs. Were they Dads or Grandpa's – we never found out. On the top of each sock a handwritten note had been pegged with almost unrecognisable handwriting 'To Judy / Sue, from Santa'. Judy sat at one end of her bed examining the tiny presents. I sat at the other end, greedy little hands tugging out the parcels from my stocking. "Look, I've got a tangerine," I cried, "And it's wrapped in silver foil." "Oooo, so have I," she replied, adding, "How does Santa know we love tangerines at Christmas?" "And chocolates too," I cried, as my hand delved deeper into the stocking. "Oh, such pretty beads" I said, as my fingers moved over the plastic beads on the necklace. "And soap too – mauve and carved out like a delicate shoe," I cried. Judy replied, her voice full of excitement, "Look, I've got a soap too and mine is pink, my favourite colour....and on a rope, Oh, it's so pretty," she squealed. Every tiny present was met by joyous screams and shrieks from Judy and I. Daylight was now flooding into our bedroom – Christmas Day had begun.

* * * * *

Judy and I sat on the carpet beside the Christmas tree gazing up at Mum. It was December 1960. "I have an extra special present for you both," Mum said. I immediately rummaged around the nearby parcels saying, "Where is it, where, Mummy, where?" Judy continued looking at Mum, now and then glancing at the wrapped presents by the tree, her eyes bright with expectation. "Girls, girls, I don't mean that sort of present," said Mum laughing. She picked up one of the decorations from the sideboard – a plastic model of Mary and Joseph sitting in a dark brown stable. The model had a very steep pyramid shaped roof with a star at the top. Placing it on the floor she pointed at the model. Looking intently at us she said, "Now who remembers the special Christmas story I told you about?" Judy looked puzzled until I blurted out, "It's the manger with Mary and Joseph and baby Jesus, isn't that right Mummy? Do I get a present from Santa now for guessing right?" "No girls," cried Mum as she sat down on the floor and wrapped her arms around her children who quickly responded by hugging her. Talking softly, she said, "Baby Jesus was the present to the world and my special present to you is that I'm having another baby." Mum prodded her bulging tummy with both her hands on her stomach – smoothing out the folds of her voluminous tent dress we could now see the huge baby mound. Both of us children erupted with gleeful shrieks and much chattering amongst ourselves. I looked at Mum, then at Judy who nodded to me. "But we want a baby brother. You must bring home a brother for us." I said solemnly. Judy banged her arms onto her thighs and piped in too with a high-pitched wail, "Not another girl, only a baby brother". A few months later Mum had her new arrival and returned from the hospital with the present that Susan and Judy had asked for - she was mightily thankful that somebody had answered her prayers.

* * * * *

Ping, woosh, and then the sound of breaking glass. I ran into the living room, Judi scampering behind, both wondering what the commotion was. Tibby, our new kitten was sitting on his hind legs and swiping at a bauble with her paw. Every now and then a glitzy ball would fly off a branch onto the carpet and Tibby would chase it around the base of the tree. Pine needles littered the floor as more glittering baubles and tinsel succumbed to Tibby's game. Mum appeared to see what the noise was. "Stop it, stop it Tibby," she yelled as she bent down to try and catch the kitten. A minute later Tibby hurtled through the open kitchen door leaving a trail of pine needles behind her. We all gaped at the base of the tree. In amongst a tangle of wrapped presents, slithers of coloured tinsel were mixed around pieces of shattered glass baubles and other tree decorations. Pine needles were everywhere. An hour later Mum finished clearing up the mess, although days later we still found the odd pine needle stubbornly lodged somewhere in the carpet. Every year from then the tree was Tibby proofed – none of us were allowed to put any decorations below Tibby's height.

* * * * *

Dad burst into our playroom, his arm was outstretched and, in his hand, he clutched a piece of white cardboard. Judy and I looked up, anxious to know what the cardboard was. It was Christmastime – maybe, I thought, it was a Christmas card. "It's arrived," he said, "Remember I told you two about my office children's Christmas party, and Santa Claus will be there too." He waived the white card in the air before placing it on our table. With a beaming face, he said, "Well, you are both invited – just look at this special invitation." With our noses almost on the table, both us girls were eagerly scanning the piece of white card; it had gold edges with images of holly sprigs at each corner with fancy writing including 'Dear Susan and Judith'. Mum came into our playroom to see her two girls jumping up and down, unable to contain their excitement. "New frocks for you both," she said. "And Dad and I will take you up to London, on (she paused) the... Big Train." Judy and I ran around the room, shrieking and yelling at the top of our voices, "We're going on the Big Train to Dads office party, we're going on the Big Train to London." Throughout this commotion little Stephen remained asleep, curled up like a ball, on the easy chair.

Going on the big train was a treat. Dad carefully lifted us, one at a time, into the carriage. When it was my turn, he noticed my hesitation as I stared at the huge gap between the platform and train step. Picking me up quickly he lifted me into the carriage before I'd had time to think about falling under the train. An hour later we arrived at a massive office block, we saw loads of other children, with their parents also holding their hands tightly. We made our way to the party. Fun, games, endless food, paper hats and brightly coloured streamers everywhere. Then we got to meet Santa Claus, who gave us a present. "But Mum," I sniffled on the train home, "I don't want a doll, can't I have another present?" Dad could also see my hot tears beginning to trickle down my face, he took the doll out of my hands saying, "Next week I'll speak to Santa and get you another very special present. And as a treat for both you girls, because you've been so very good today, we'll get fish and chips." Instantly feeling better, I smiled at both my parents.

Susan and Judy, and hordes of other children at Dads Christmas office party.

Snow was fluttering in the dusky air as we got off the train and we all trudged wearily along the pavement to the chip shop. Clutching our hot parcels encased in yesterdays' newspaper we strode home amid the haze of yellow streetlamps and, for Judy and I, happy memories of our trip out on the Big Train.

* * * * *

"Ow, you've got my eye," said a muffled voice from beneath a blanket. I immediately pulled my hand away from the covering. Everyone in the room stopped moving, and for a moment the silence was stifling. Reeling backwards, I turned to see my Mum with a bemused look on her face. I was shaking all over and turned my gaze back to see the blanket falling to the ground. The silence gave way to laughter when we all saw a grown up holding an orange, with her finger brazenly gouging out a hole in the orange skin. We were at a neighbours Christmas party: parents and lots of over excited children. Presents from Santa, and traditional games gave way to guessing games which led onto the blanket game. Guessing the occupant under the blanket, was, for me, a Christmas party game I'd rather forget!

* * * * *

Mum made the Christmas cake every year. The smell of spices, dried fruits, sugar and brandy wound its way into our playroom, the living room, and we scurried through with wide eyes and salivating lips to find a near empty bowl waiting for us. Mum had just put the cake in the oven. Turning towards us she said, "Washing up time now. I left you some cake mixture in the bowl. Without saying a word Judy and I both clasped each side of the bowl, she pulling it one way and then I pulled it the other. "Now, don't fight, you can both share it," she said. Mum reached for the two spoons she had used to mix the cake; an old wooden spoon and a metal tablespoon. "Here," she said softly, handing a spoon to each of us. For both of us, licking the raw cake remnants was even better than tasting the cooked cake. And part of the fun was to look at each other's faces; noses, cheeks and hair, smeared with this creamy mixture.

A few days later we all took part in getting the brown spicy cake ready for Christmas. After Mum had smeared melted marmalade all over the cake and stuck a gaudy shade of yellow marzipan to it – then our skills were called upon. We took it in turns to batter the top of the cake with thick, white icing. Sometimes Mum would swirl the mixture into peaks "Just like snow drifts" she'd say. Next, she'd wrap a red and white frieze around the cake and seal the ends with sewing pins. Inside a large Tupperware box was a collection of ceramic Christmas cake decorations; often they had been thrown into the box the year before still coated with white powdery icing on their base. I dipped my hands in first to find Santa. He was our favourite decoration; bright red tunic and big white beard flowing down to his waist. I plonked him in position, and his feet stuck firm to Mums snow. Judy pulled out the toboggan – it was just like the sledge Dad had made us. Then the red postbox (with a robin nestling on top), a wire Christmas tree with white blobs of snow on the tips – that punctured into the cake and finally the Merry Christmas sign. Dad congratulated us all when he came home from work that evening, as he did every year. From Christmas Day the cake began shrinking as we began to devour it. A week after Christmas only a quarter was left – with all the cake decorations fighting for a place on the remaining piece. A few days later the icing coated decorations were thrown in their box, and forgotten about until next Christmastime.

5 Old Crocks Race: Prams and Lampshades

The morning air was cold. As I held my dad's hand, waiting for something to happen, I practiced seeing how far my puffs of breath could reach out in front of me. They lingered in the crisp air and then snaked away, at almost a yard, into oblivion. We all stood along the hard pavement: Mum – gently rocking Stephen as he lay in his pram, Dad, Judy and I, some of our neighbour's, and many strangers – old and young. Rows of people dressed up in thick coats and scarves, with children wearing mittens and wellies to keep out the November chill and occasional rain spits. I let out another loud 'phew' and was about to watch my breath race through the air when my Dad tugged briskly on my duffle coat sleeve, "Susan, look, the next car is coming. Stop fooling around and look at the car," he said in a stern voice.

We were all standing on a freezing cold pavement at Gatton Bottom, along the A23, the main road between London and Brighton, not that I knew that then – it was the big road that we hardly ever saw, right on the edge of us children's 'world'. Suddenly I heard a hissing sound accompanied by a clock ticking loudly, or so I thought. A regular clank, clank, clank sound filled the autumn air. I leaned round a coat standing in front of me – annoyed that an adult was blocking my view of the approaching sight. Dad had told me about these cars that had been made in the olden days. And they were nothing like the modern-day mass-produced flashy Zepha 6 that our flashy neighbours had, let alone our little blue Ford Anglia which had also been churned out on a production line. Dad had said that the cars were not racing each other between London and Brighton.

The event was just a parade of vintage vehicles, many of which never completed the route. And that many of the people taking part even wore Victorian or Edwardian costumes to make the whole event much more authentic. I peered around the grey flannel coat flap and its wearer, who sensed my presence, he shifted to one side.

I gasped at the sight in front of me. The vehicle had clunked to a halt a few yards from me. Steam was bellowing from the engine and every now and then a huge extra jet of steamy water spurted into the air. This machine didn't look like a car to me – it looked like a huge luxurious motorised pram. The "pram" had no fixed roof just a tiny glass windscreen and it was red and shiny with gold framed mirrors and ornate headlamps and horn. And the wheels looked like they belonged to a posh bicycle. Both the cloth capped driver and his elegant female companion vacated the 'pram' and began pulling up a canopy – to me, it looked like they were unfolding the hood of a pram so it would enclose the car and keep out the drizzle. Before the woman stepped back inside the car, she walked towards us onlookers. She twirled and then curtsied so low I could almost touch the long feathers on her magnificent hat, and then she waved her lace gloved hands and held her parasol majestically in the air before disappearing back inside the pram. The man scurried round to the hissing engine and was soon joined by what Dad called "the back-up troops" – men who knew a thing or two about how to get a broken engine get going again. Moments later the hissing and smelly spluttering stopped, and the troops, who, I thought, didn't look like khaki- clad soldiers, carried on tinkering with the engine.

One of the men appeared to be putting a spanner into the engine grill and began winding it up like a clock.

Dad could see the look of puzzlement on my face – "That's a crank," he said, "Like a large key to wind it up like a clockwork toy to start the engine." A moment later the vehicle moved forwards, stopped, then carried on its journey. The 'troops' melted into the crowded pavement. All that was left behind was a strong smell of engine oil and a momentary silence as many hands went back in their coat pockets until the next cars came into view. Quickly a whole fleet of veteran cars emerged from the mist and trundled along the road towards us. When each car passed, we all waved and cheered and some of the car occupants waved back too. Judy jumped up and down in excitement. I soon followed her example, totally unaware that I was bouncing towards the grey flannel coat and my outstretched arms were also knocking into the other coats around me. Dad then picked me up so my head was at his head-height, almost nose to nose. I really thought a telling off was coming, but in the next moment Mum intervened and said to her husband, "Andrew, I think we've all had enough excitement for one day, let's go home. And hot sweet cocoa to drink for everyone." Dad beamed widely as he gently lifted me to pavement level, patting me on the head. I looked up at his still smiling face and said, "Dad, please can I have my cocoa in the garden?" Almost at the same moment, Judy cried out, "And I want cocoa in the garden too." Both parents grinned at each other. The promise of cocoa always won the day.

Some-time later I kept remembering the elegant lady, the passenger in the red pram. Us children were playing with our toys in the living room. I twirled around, flung out my arms and pretended to curtsey.

Susan drinking cocoa in the garden.

* * * * *

“What are you doing?” said Judy in a rather disinterested voice – she barely lifted her head to glance at me. “I’m pretending to be that lady we saw yesterday,” I said, “You remember the lady who got out of the car and twirled around right in front of us.” Judy thought for a moment, obviously remembered and then thundered out of the room and up the stairs. I could hear her footsteps on the floor of the room above. “What was she doing in Mum and Dads room?” I wondered. She reappeared through the lounge door, out of breath, and dragging a large cream coloured canvas bag by its thick drawstrings. “The dressing up bag,” I exclaimed, “Why didn’t I think of that!.” Judy glared at me, “You didn’t,” she said, “I did.” And then stuck out her tongue in my direction.

The old canvas bag was like an old army kitbag, maybe Grandpa’s. And it was now stuffed full of old clothes that we’d use to dress up in: Mums, Granny’s and other relatives’ castoffs including patterned dresses, silk scarves, sequinned blouses, long billowy skirts, squashed hats, sparkling jewellery and a riot of coloured beads. Judy was first to dive into the enormous bag pulling out dresses and exotic looking necklaces. I grabbed a lace blouse, and carried on rummaging through the bag until I found a flowing skirt. Giggling loudly as we attempted to put on the huge clothes, we had obviously caught Mums attention as her head appeared around the kitchen door. She looked at Judy and I, then the mess of clothes on the carpet and the near empty dressing up bag lying forlornly by the sofa. Then, her shoulders appeared around the door, quickly followed by the rest of her body. “What are you both doing?” she said. “We’re pretending to be the lady we saw yesterday in the old red car,” I said, as I energetically twirled around the room. Momentarily stopping and out of breath, I looked up and said, “But I need a hat, she had a beautiful hat – Mum, I can't find one." As always, Mum came to the rescue. She began by looking through the abandoned clothes on the carpet with her nimble-fingered hands, and then rifled through what was left in the kit-bag. "Here it is," she said, as she pulled out a knitted cream-coloured hat. "This was your Granny's cloche hat – will that do," she asked. I looked at the object, it was flat, shapeless and not at all what I wanted. "But," I said, "It has to have feathers, and be brightly coloured...and ladylike." My eyes, then my head, then my shoulders drooped before I started crying. Mums' arms reached out, encircled my body, wiped away my hot tears and then she hugged me. "Susan, I think we may have just what you are looking for," she said softly. Standing up, she walked into the hall. I could hear the latch open on the understairs cupboard. A minute or two later she came into the lounge carrying a red object. Bending down to me she said, "Here it is, one of our old red lampshades, we were going to throw them out. Look at the lovely red satin fabric and all those gold-coloured tassels – just like feathers," she proclaimed. She shook the lampshade and the long tassels began to look like floating feathers. "A real lady would look so beautiful wearing this" she said with a smile. Mum carefully fixed the lampshade on my head, and I twirled, and the long gold tassels danced then hovered in the air. "What about me," cried Judy, "It was me who got the dressing up bag, it was my idea. I want a lampshade hat too" she shouted at Mum and I. Judy then attempted to knock me over, her arms pushing into my body. But, as I was older and heavier than her, I remained standing. Judy started biting my arm instead. I screamed, "It's my h...," I yelled." "It was my" ... (idea), she bellowed back. I tried to shriek back, "It was my ....". "No it...," she bellowed. The noise was deafening as we both shouted over each other.

An exasperated Mum pushed us apart – one little girl each side of her. “Stop squabbling you two. If you want to look like a lady, you must behave like a lady,” she said in a gentle but firm tone of voice. She shook her head and frowned, and then walked back to the hall. I heard the latch open again, and some rummaging before she came back triumphantly carrying a second red lampshade and placed it on Judy’s tiny head. With a smile, echoed by her two girls, mum then exclaimed, “Pretty as a picture,” as she watched her children shaking their lampshade covered heads to watch the delicate long gold tassels elegantly drifting in the air like feathers.

* * * * *

A few years later, while on one of our West Country holidays, we children found our very own motorised prams – just like the old crocks. And they were covered with pram hoods too, to keep out the rain, and a tooting horn which resembled a trombone with a cricket ball at one end. “Please can we have a go Dad, please, please,” we three children said. Dad could see the enthusiasm on our faces as we tugged his pullover to get his attention. Smiling he said, “Alright then, but two at a time.” Stephen, being a boy, decided he ought to drive the motorised pram. Dad helped him into the vehicle and there he sat, proudly behind the steering wheel and raring to go. I clambered in beside him. I stretched out my arm to squeeze the cricket ball hooter – it worked, so I carried on loudly letting everyone know that we were in the pram. “We’re off,” said Stephen, as he excitingly grabbed the steering wheel. We drove for what seemed like miles and miles, not really noticing or caring that we were actually going round and round in circles on a vintage car merry-go-round.

Susan and Stephen on merry-go-round.

* * * * *

6 Sweet Shoes

"Ooo Mum, can I have some" I said as I peered through the shop window; my nose pressed heavily against the glass. My hand wiped away the condensation I'd created and I carried on looking at the delicious colours. Turning around to face Mum, I looked up - my eyes glinted and a mischievous smile ran right across my face. I pulled Mums hand so she stood nearer the shop window. "Please can I have some," I cried, my voice raised in anticipation. The sweetshop, the Bon Bon, was on our route home from school. Moments later, and still holding Mums hand, I almost dragged her into the shop. The small sweetshop had row upon row of shelves, all filled with shiny glass jars stuffed full of sweets; and a sugary sweet smell lingered in the air. I stood at the wooden counter looking up at a stack of cream paper bags; brand new and waiting to be filled. Beyond this, the silver-coloured cash register had just been opened by the shopkeeper. I looked up at him, he smiled down at me saying "Won't be a moment." Mum crouched down beside me and said, "As a treat I'll let you have some today, but we must save some for your sister". "Oh, but..." I retorted, not wanting to share my sweets. I gazed again at the shelves on every wall; all the colours of the rainbow swimming around my head. Vibrant colours and amazing flavours – I remembered them all. My eyes grew wider as I tried to take in the delights before me. I felt my arm being shaken. "Susan, Susan," said Mum, "Have you decided yet?" I shook my tilted head towards the floor. "No, er, um, I don't know," I blurted out. "I like them all." "Well," said Mum, "I think we should go for flying saucers and licorice allsorts – you and Judy always like them." The shopkeeper overheard Mum and then looked at me. Although I nodded in agreement, he could already see by the wide smile on my face that I agreed. Our sweets were weighed and put in paper bags for Mum to carry. Before the shop door had closed behind us I tugged at her skirt and cried “Can I have a flying saucer…..please Mum.” She knew I loved the sherbet-filled spheres. I popped the rice paper object in my mouth and sucked – the sherbet seemed to explode in the roof of my mouth leaving a sharp sugary taste which oozed down my throat. We carried on walking – I now had a spring in my step. Turning to me she said, “And did you have a good day at school today?” With my sherbet flavoured mouth still tickling I coughed and mumbled, “Oh thesss.”

* * * * *

“Susan, Judy,” cried Mum, “Hold my hand - we need to cross the road.” It was mid-afternoon and the summer heat was still intense as we walked home from my school. A moment later, Mum turned her head to see her young girls still calmly ambling along the gritty footpath and singing to themselves. “Susan, Judy, come here,” said Mum, her voice slightly raised and her cheeks reddened. Rows of semi-detached houses lined both sides of the quiet road. One of the favourite pastimes of us youngsters as we walked home from school was peering into the front gardens of these houses; over a low wall or through a hedge. “Girls, stop being so nosy,” exclaimed Mum as she gripped our hands tightly as we crossed the road. Judy and I continued our snooping, much to Mums annoyance, until the pavement widened, and inclined upwards to the parade of shops. I looked back over the road and fixed my eyes on the Post Office. “Mum, can we go there, I like going in the Post Office cos they sell the best Scraps, pleeease,” I cried as I skipped back down the pavement. “We’ll go another day, you know it’s new shoes day,” replied Mum in a firm tone.

Annoyed, I pulled my school beret off my head and threw it at Mum. Running back up the pavement I glared at Mum as I overtook her and Judy.

I arrived at the shoe shop first, my irritation soon forgotten. Standing underneath the shop front canopy and by the entrance step I lifted one foot onto the step and hesitated; at nearly seven-years-old I was not yet bold enough to go in on my own. "Come on you two, in we go," puffed Mum as she patted our backs and pushed us in; she was still clutching my school beret. We entered a dimly lit room – a welcome coolness unlike the hot temperatures outside. I gazed at the back wall. Each side of a brightly lit open doorway I saw rows of orderly shelves with a huge number of neatly stacked boxes of shoes; adult shoes I assumed as the cardboard boxes were mainly large. Mesmerised, I barely saw the shape of the shopkeeper emerge from the doorway at the back of the dark and gloomy shop. "Good afternoon, shoes for the children?" he said looking directly at Mum. Judy and I both sidled up to Mum, almost hiding behind the folds in her skirt. "Sit down, sit down, please," said the shopkeeper as he ushered us all to a row of wooden chairs. Judy and I sat patiently while the adults talked for some while.

Moments later, "So you are Susan," said the smiling shopkeeper. He pointed to the corner of the room, "Come my dear, I've got a very special machine for you to stand on – it measures your feet by taking an X-ray." My eyes followed the direction of his arm. I then looked up at Mum, my lips were pursed, shoulders hunched forwards. I carried on perching on my seat, my little legs dangled inches from the carpet – each leg increasingly rocking up and down. Mum saw my agitation and put her arm around me. "I'll walk over with you to the machine", Mum whispered softly putting her other arm

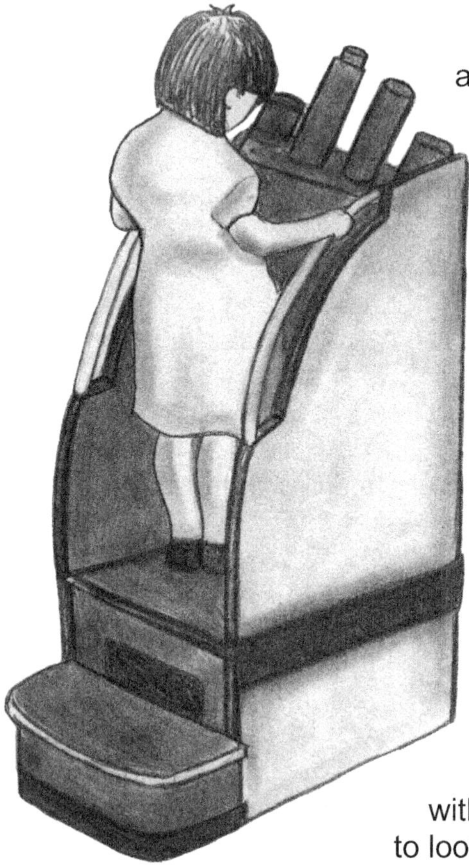

around me. Adding, "You need to take your shoes off, but not your socks." Feeling the warmth and softness of the carpet through my socks, I stepped up to the wooden box. I was almost as tall as the wooden machine. The shopkeeper then pointed at the bottom and said gently, "If you step up to that ledge, yes that's right, and put both your feet into that cubby hole." I looked at the dark cubby hole, began to put my foot space, then quickly withdrew it. Turning my head to look at Judy I noticed the frightened look on her face. Mum intervened saying, "It's okay, the machine will only be taking a picture of your feet." I gulped hard and thrust one foot and then the other into the cavernous box. Mum continued to hold my clammy hand, every now and then squeezing it to reassure me. The adults looked through the vision panels at the top of the box and both nodded in agreement. Mum squeezed my hand again. A button was pressed, and the wooden box juddered into life. "Look up Susan," said Mum – her arm outstretched and the other hand holding my chin up towards the ceiling. A light flashed and the machine made a clicking sound. "There you are, all done," said the shopkeeper. He and Mum shepherded me back to the safety of the row of chairs and I noticed the petrified figure of Judy. She was clinging on tightly to the chair arms, shrieking "No Mummy, no, no, no Mumm...ey." "It's alright Judy" Mum murmured as she put her arm around Judy's squirming body, "You don't need to go on the machine if you don't want to."

The shopkeeper bent down and pulled a flimsy black sheet from the back of the machine and disappeared through the door at the back of the shop. Minutes later he emerged holding a small cardboard box in one hand and a shoehorn in the other. "This should be the perfect size for you," he grinned. I looked down at the open box, watching him unravel the tissue paper. "Your Mum tells me you like red, what do you think of these?" I nodded my head, my mouth opened, my eyes shone brightly, I breathed in slowly through my nose; the aroma of brand-new leather was powerful. The red shoes fitted me like a glove. I wore them for 'occasions', unlike the next pair Mum bought me, school shoes – black, sturdy and functional. Over the next months and few years using the X-ray machine became a highlight for Judy and I during several of our walks home from school.

* * * * *

7 Sound and Little Screen

On a hot, but wet summers day all three children were in the living room of their home. "Mum, Mum, when can we watch Watch with Mother," cried Judy. Her rag doll was lying abandoned on the carpet along with other toys scattered here and there. The outside rain beat noisily on the window panes, as it had done all morning. All three children were bored – not liking being confined to the airless house. Susan stomped around the living room, glanced at the rain spattered windows, then at the sleeping body of baby Stephen lying on the sofa surrounded by springy cushions. Mum looked at her girls' despondent faces and then at the clock on the wall. "Yes, it's nearly time for Watch with Mother," she said while she held out her arms towards both of her girls. She sat Judy on the carpet, knelt beside her and wrapped her arms around her tiny frame. Turning her head towards her other daughter, "Susan," she said, "Can you turn the knob on for the TV, then we can all watch together." After a while, grainy images appeared on the tiny screen on the huge brown box. "And turn up the sound knob please," she added. After a few crackles, a female voice was heard; "Andy Pandy's come to play, la, la, la," as the opening sequence began. Susan, at just over five years old, yelled out the letters as they appeared on the screen – "A, N, D, Y, and P, and A, N, D, and Y," she shrieked at the top of her voice. Stephen remained unconscious to the noise of Susan's high-pitched yells.

At certain times every week the children, and sometimes with their friends too, would escape into the TV world of these puppets; the main character being Andy Pandy who sported a vivid striped all-in-one suit with a huge white ruff around his neck. His friend Teddy, a teddy bear, and Looby Loo – a rag-doll who wore a polka dot dress and would only spring to life when Andy and Teddy were not around.

Susan and Judy waited, holding their breath for a few seconds; their eyes fixed on the tiny black and white screen in front of them.

A picnic basket appeared, the lid slowly lifted and the crumpled figures of Andy Pandy and Teddy popped up to wave to the audience. The children waved back, entranced by the marionettes as they bobbed up and down to the simple storyline. At the end of this adventure both puppets climbed up and into their basket. "Oh, they are going," wailed Judy who promptly began sucking her thumb. Music followed, a narrator started singing, "Time to go home, time to go home, Andy is waving goodbye, goodbye." The hollow silence of both girls was interrupted by the squeals and cries of baby Stephen as he woke from his slumbers.

* * * * *

Some months later, us children were swathed in long socks and winter cardi's, we listened to the noise coming from the old black and white TV set echoing around the living room – "Bill and Ben, Flowerpot men, Flowerpot men" sang the narrator accompanied by the plip plop plip of a xylophone. "Plip plop flip, Bill and Ben, Bill and Ben, plip plop flip"..... Spellbound, we all sat silently on the snug carpet watching the puppets as they juddered up and down. "Flibadobs, flobadobs, flibadobs" warbled the identical figures as they popped up from two flowerpots, hidden from the real world behind an old potting shed. Each puppet was made from a big flowerpot for the body, smaller pots stacked down their long spindly legs to their hobnail boots, with rubber gardening gloves for each hand. The puppet strings were clearly visible to adults, but we children only saw two little dancing men and their friend – Little Weed whose flower head nodded in time to the beat of the xylophone; "Plip, plop, flip, plip, plop, flip."

Mum was listening from the kitchen; she heard shrieks of laughter and knew the puppets were up to mischief. Sure enough, the xylophone "Plip plopped" slowly as a female voice-over sang, "Was it Bill or was it Ben?" More shrieks and squeals reverberated through the open door. "It was Bill" screamed Judy. Mum stood by the connecting kitchen door watching her children; she had a broad smile across her face. Susan was still kneeling on the carpet; her hands were clasped over her headand her eyes gaping intently at the screen. Judy was now standing, her agitated arms outstretched and pointing towards the puppets. Stephen, propped up by cushions, was sitting upright, with his chubby fingers banging loudly against the string of rubber toys fastened across his pram. More high-pitched yelps and then silence as a shrill, loud voice rang out, "Weeeeeeeeed." "It's Little Weed," cried Judy. "Oh, quick, quick, quick, hide – the Gardener is coming," yelled Judy. Moments later the closing sequence of the programme began – "Goodbye Bill, goodbye Ben." Mum stepped into the living room. "Teas ready you three, and mind you two girls don't stampede in here like a heard of elephants!"

* * * * *

The following year and on another wet afternoon, Susan cried "Ooo, look at their big ears," as two puppet pigs moved up and down beside a table. "They look like elephant ears," added Judy, chuckling out loud. Pinky and Perky carried on juddering and moving around the breakfast table. Their voices set them apart from other children's programmes on TV at that time – the puppets high-pitched squeal sounded just like playing a gramophone record at twice the normal speed. Mum was sitting on the floor with her children watching too: "Which pig is Pinky and which is Perky," she asked. Thrusting her arm up and waving her hand in the air, six-year-old Susan who had just learnt to do this at school, then shoved Judy in the small of her back and bellowed in a superior tone, "Pinky hasn't got a hat on and Perky has." "I knew that too," screamed Judy as she turned around to punch Susan's arm. "Stop fighting children, look, they are going to sing a song," said Mum in her stern voice. High pitched squeals emanated from the TV screen accompanied by the equally piercing tones of the children as they sang along with the dancing marionettes. A few years later the squeals of Pinky and Perky were still just as popular with the children. Susan and Judy particularly, would often mimic the pig's voices whether they were watching them on TV or at random moments during the day. And always accompanied by a rising crescendo of the girl's giggling.

Singing along to Pinky and Perky's version of The Beatles "All My Loving" on the BBC's Duke Box Jury – "Is the record a Hit or a Miss?" led the girls to discover The Hit Parade - all the popular songs of the day. One day a blue and cream coloured tartan box appeared – Dad took it into the lean-to beside the kitchen. It was rather like a small suitcase with two big metal clips and a carrying handle. Dad opened up the box with a click, click, "This is a record player," he said. All three children peered at the turntable, stylus arm and knobs in awe – none really knowing what did what. That Saturday Susan and Judy spent their pocket money on their first gramophone records. In the gramophone shop they stood beside Dad looking at the weekly list of the Hit Parade. Their fingers ran up and down the list, "I'll have this one, no that one," said Susan who settled on a song – The Moody Blues "Go Now." Judy decided on Tom Jones "It's not unusual". Once home those first gramophone records were played endlessly all day long and hearing Mum shouting "Your lunch is ready" or "Teas ready" was the only way to stop the din!

* * * * *

"It's a bear," screamed Judi. "A talking bear," yelled Susan. Even young Stephen joined in, "Look, look, look," he said with a raised voice and then promptly collapsed on the carpet in a fit of giggles. Moments earlier all three children had sat sedately on the grey and maroon pinstriped sofa. Mum and Dad were also watching this Saturday night variety show on the TV with their children. Andy Williams was a popular entertainer and his cosy innocuous songs entertained family audiences in the 1960s, including our family. The bear looked very life like and us children believed the 6-foot-high creature was real. Of course, our parents knew otherwise but didn't spoil our excitement. "Mum," yelled Judy, "The bear is asking Andy Williams for some milk and cookies. Look, look. Oh, the bear is holding a glass of milk." Us three children were transfixed – the American TV show seemed so much more alive than most of the British variety shows, I thought. "He wants cookies," exclaimed Judy. "And so do I," she added whilst turning her head to look at Mum. "And me, me, me," cried Stephen. Not to be left out I joined in too with the chanting, "Cookies, cookies, we want cookies," we all shrieked. Dad stood up, walked to the TV set and hovered with his finger above the on/off button. "Enough of that din, all three of you sit down properly and watch the TV," he said with a cross look on his face. Mum intervened, always the peacemaker, "As a special treat, and if you all behave yourselves," she said slowly as she looked at all her three children. "Why don't we all make some cookies tomorrow," she said. Dad nodded in agreement and rejoined us on the sofa. By now the TV show had moved onto a song and dance routine and we all sat engrossed by the brightly coloured costumes and dancing spectacular. But, at the end of the programme all I was thinking about was cookies. And day-dreaming about the sweet smell and taste of the mixture we'd be making on Sunday. Cooked and licking the bowl of the uncooked cookie mixture was equally delicious to children with a sweet tooth!

* * * * *

8 Lollipops, Echoes and Brownies

Susan and Judy lingered at the top of the pathway; Judy's hands holding the black iron railings beside the school gate, her bright eyes peering down the hillside. The older children bounced past them, crying out in glee, "Home time, I'll race you to the shops, no more school." Little ones trudged slowly down the path to the crossing, just happy that the gradient was downhill. Up above, the sound of singing and laughter in the playground by excited children echoed in the air. The embankment from the primary school was steep down to the road, a tarmac pathway zig-zagged left then right through all the dense greenery on the hillside. School Hill hadn't changed much in hundreds of years; the road connecting Old Merstham to South Merstham.

The gouged-out road inclined down the middle of the hill, beyond the wooden fences on both sides of the road which separated the road and footpath. The bank rose steeply on either side. The primary school was located on the west side; the main entrance, on foot, was accessed via School Hill. A crowd of children and mothers with pushchairs and prams were standing on the levelled-off pathway, youngsters straining against the iron railings, voices hushed as they waited to cross the road. All of them watching the authority of the new lollipop lady; she strode out into the road, her white coat flapping around her knees as the wind rustled down the hill. She held her sign at arms-length, thrusting it up towards the sky – waiting for the traffic to stop before placing the pole down on the road surface and beckoning the group to venture into the road. Children and adults spewed out into the road; some walked slowly, others jostled as they dashed to the other side of the road.

As the lollipop lady walked briskly back to the school side of the road, Susan smiled at her saying, “Hello Mum, we’ll wait here - until you’ve finished.” An autumn chill was in the air; the two young girls huddled together as more cold wind came down the hill; each girl pulling their scarves tighter and turning their backs to the cold wind. Another large group of children appeared, then a few minutes later the final stragglers crossed the road and vanished down the hill. Mum took her lollipop sign and white coat back to the school and rejoined her girls. Susan and Judy held Mums hands tightly, as they waited to cross the road. A car suddenly came into view, hurtling up the hill - the railway bridge had obscured all vision and softened sounds of approaching vehicles. “Goodness, this is dangerous,” cried Mum – aware that both her girls were gripping her hands more tightly. Looking one way and then the other in quick succession, Mum, not hearing or seeing any traffic, the three of them almost ran across the road to begin the walk home from school. After a few months Mum gave up being a lollipop lady - even the school headmaster admitted to her that it was not safe. She soon found another part-time job.

* * * * *

“Hello oh,” shouted Susan. She strained her head upwards for the reply. Underneath the bridge at the bottom of School Hill a distinct “Hello oh,” echoed back. Giggling, Judy joined in, “Hello Susan,” she shouted. The dark bridge echoed back, “Hello Susan.” Under the low arch of the bridge the black bricks were covered with slime, the air was dank – sunshine never found its way beneath this bridge. Susan shivered and ran to the other side to feel the Autumn sun warm her body. There were five bridges between school and home, and the two girls delighted in creating echoes under these brick echo chambers. The two girls rushed ahead as Mum walked to the zebra crossing – located underneath a second railway bridge. No good for echoes Susan thought as it was tall, square and narrow.

Both girls held Mums hands as they all crossed the road. Susan ran ahead to the next bridge – fifty yards from the crossing; the underside of the bridge roof bricks was even blacker with small channels of water running down to the pavement. "Judy Puddy pudden and pie," sang Susan as she ran through the cavernous structure. "Judy Puddy pudden and pie," repeated the bridge. Just before the fourth railway bridge was an unmade-up road. In summer the mud surface had turned to dust, littered with shingle and sharp-edged stones. Now, the earlier rain had left the road pitted with water-filled craters of varying sizes. And in winter, when the girls wore their wellington boots to school, they'd jump into the deep puddles cascading water in all directions, including their clothes. Mum's reprimands often resulted in them not walking on that side of the pavement for a few days. Passing under the fifth railway bridge was even more hazardous than the first bridge. It was on a sharp double bend; the road was narrow with only just enough space for a path on one side. Mum and her two girls walked around the road as it swung abruptly to the right, their steps slightly faltering as all eyes scanned the unfolding scene ahead. Mum sighed in relief; no traffic. Susan and Judy let go of Mums hands. They strode under the low arch of the railway bridge - the sound of joyous "Hello, hello's" rang out in the air. The last echo chamber had been conquered.

* * * * *

"Stephen, Oh, you've come to meet us from school," I exclaimed. "And on the sledge too," added Judy. We

Susan & Judy pulling Stephen on sledge.

both wrapped our arms around him, hugging and laughing with him. The three-year-old made gurgling and clucking noises while throwing his head back and forth – the huge grin on his face getting wider and wider. That winter a thick layer of snow had descended on much of the country, including our village. Mum, forever resourceful, had brought Stephen on the new sledge that Dad had made for us. Stephen sat on the wooden sledge, his stubby hands wrapped around its metal handles, while Mum pulled a piece of rope attached to the sledge so it glided along the snow. Much of the school route was flat – even up to our road. Of course, Stephen had to get off every time we all crossed a road - his little legs buried in snow, and Mum clinging onto his hand whilst attempting to hold the slippery wooden sledge with her remaining free hand. At least on the way home there were two extra pairs of hands to help with this task! And when we got home, we were allowed to carry on playing in the snow, pulling Stephen back and forth on the sledge – all three of us laughing hysterically as Tibby, our cat, tried to join in the fun too.

* * * * *

"That's where I go to Brownies," I cried, holding my head up as high as I could and pointing my hand towards a building. We'd just passed the shops, turned right at the junction and looked across the road at All Saints Church - beyond the church was a hall. I had stopped on the pavement. I grabbed Judy's arm, turning her around to look at the hall. "See, there, that's where I go to Brownies," I shouted with an air of superiority. My little sister was not impressed. She pulled away from me and held Mums hand as the three of us stared at Canada Hall. My head was filled with thrilling memories of my first visit – only a few days ago. "I'm getting my own uniform," I persisted. "Yes, I know darling," said Mum, "Dad and I are very proud of you." Turning to my sister, I said, "Brenda Brown Owl says I'll be in the Pixie group and I can earn lots of badges." Judy was standing to one side of Mum; she stuck her tongue out at me and then buried her head between the folds of Mums skirt. I began to put out my arm to hit Judy, Mum grabbed my hand, saying to us both, "Children, please, no bickering." Mum was watching me as I opened my mouth to protest. Interrupting and in a soothing voice she murmured to both of us, "We're nearly halfway home now – would you like your favourite for tea tonight?" "Oh yes please," we both called out. Judy and I smiled, although not at each other, and skipped along the pathway till we got home.

* * * * *

To me, going to Brownie's became a passion. A few months after my introduction to Brownie's I was so proud to be a Brownie. I loved my uniform – a plain brown shift dress (over the coming years the front was covered by badges), leather belt, useful tie and woollen beret. Every week me and my fellow Brownie's would stand in a line, waiting nervously for Brenda Brown Owl to inspect us. I thought I had put on all the uniform meticulously, but our

Leader always found the minute detail that wasn't quite right. "Susan," she'd say, "Your tie is too far up from your belt by ½ inch – can you re-fold it now." I soon learnt what attention to detail meant. Scuffed shoes were another no no. At home I would spend ages sitting on the carpeted floor, with an opened tin of brown greasy shoe polish and a brown stained duster in my hand rubbing vigorously at my shoes until I could see my reflection in each shiny shoe. Mum soon banned me from doing this inside the house as I had left tell- tale brown smudges on the carpet, door frames and marks all over my fingers and hands as well as my clothes. "What's darning?" I asked Mum, one afternoon. "Says in my handbook – learn the importance of darning skills," I said with a puzzled look; my wide-open eyes looking up at Mum for an explanation. She laughed and looked down at my ankles. Smiling, she said, "You know you are often wearing out your socks and holes appear, and then I patch up the hole by weaving wool, like a tapestry, in and out of each strand. Then the sock is as good as new and can be used for a few more months." I pursed my lips, continued looking puzzled. A moment later I pulled off my shoe, tugged and twisted my sock until the ankle area revealed a hole held together with strands of wool – a slightly different colour than the rest of the sock. "Oh yes," I squealed, "Mum, can you teach me how to do darning? Please, please, then I can get another Badge." A few months later Granny tried to teach me how to knit. Dropped stitches, wrong stitches and holes, not to mention Granny's tested patience, I did succeed. Eventually I got my Knitters badge to add to the Homemaker badge – as I had finally learnt how to be clean and tidy around the house, much to Mums relief.

Proud Susan wearing her brownie uniform.

No more stray clothes left around my bedroom, no more of my toys scattered around the house, and me asking to help Mum, rather than her asking me ten times over to do many of the 100's of chores she did everyday around the home – "Thank you for doing that, Susan," she said cheerfully. "I was going to ask, but I see you've already done it," she'd say to me regularly.

Time passed, Judy was now a Brownie and I was about to join a Guide unit. "Mummy, Mummy," yelled Judy, as she hurtled into the kitchen. "Susan said she is flying up to Guides," she exclaimed, while tugging Mums skirt. "Oh, please can I go with her, Oh, Oh, I've never been on a plane, and I want to, Mummy, Mummy, please," she shouted. Judy was bouncing around Mum, flinging her arms in the air with excitement. Mum grasped Judy's arms saying, "Calm down, that's right, calm down." She slid a chair out from beneath the kitchen table, "Just sit on that chair and let me tell you all about it," she said. Judy obediently sat on the chair and looked up at Mum with huge expectant eyes, mumbling "a plane, flying on a real plane." Mum sighed, sat next to Judy and put her arm around Judy's shoulder. She then explained that "Flying up (to Guides)" was actually a ceremony and had nothing to do with aeroplanes. "In fact," said Mum, "It's a celebration of Susan's achievements, like all the badges she's worked so hard for, and the promise of what's to come as she gets older." Judy gazed around the kitchen; her eyes settled on the larder door. "You know," said Mum whose eyes had followed her young daughters gaze, "That's just what I was thinking about. And what treat would you like – a butterfly cake or maybe a piece of freshly baked flapjack?" Judy jumped off the wooden chair, her eyes sparkled, smiling, she looked up at Mum, giggled, then said, "a flying butterfly cake please."

* * * * *

"Yuk," I said, scowling and twitching my nose in response to the acrid smell and revolting taste in my mouth. I promptly downed a tin mug of cold tea before turning round to see my fellow Guides reacting in a similar way. It was the morning of my very first Guide camp and we were all sitting round the camp fire, on boxes, supposedly eating our porridge. "Sorry," said one of the Guides who was on 'cook patrol' that day, "Burnt cinders from the fire blew into the porridge pot." One of the other Guide leaders added, "Put some more sugar on your porridge." I was soon discovering that guide camp was not a big holiday; from learning how to light a fire without matches, putting up a full-size bell tent, digging trenches for our toilets, to using scavenged tree branches and making complicated string knots to construct a tripod to use as washstand, to sleeping on the grass with only a thin ground sheet and sleeping bag between me and the hard soil – whatever the challenge, we had to learn it.

"Did you enjoy camping?" shouted Mum over the din of all the excited guides who were jumping down from the back of an old and shabby farm truck. Smiling, and with the biggest grin that I could muster, I said, "Oh Mum, I had the bestest time ever." She looked at my sun tanned and dusty limbs before replying, "I did too when I was your age. Going to camp is such fun, nothing else like it – new experiences, new skills, forging deeper friendships." Grinning, she added, "And right up to my early 20's when I became a Guide leader, and then of course I didn't go on guide camps for some while." I reached out as someone passed me my, by now, well-worn kitbag. Two guides waved at me through the commotion. "Bye Janet, bye Diane," I yelled above the noise to my new found friends. Turning, I passed the bag to Mum, and said with a mystified voice, "Why didn't you continue with guide camps?" "Because," she said, first looking up to the sky in disbelief at her, at times, scatterbrained daughter, before grinning and almost laughing, "I married your father, and then you came along, and then Judy and Stephen. But, like you, I had the best time ever from Brownies and beyond." Pausing, just for a brief moment, she said quickly, "Now, let's get you back home."

* * * * *

9 Scavenging in the Hedgerows

It was half-term at school - one of my first, I was nearly six. "What would you girls like to do today," said Mum, looking expectantly at Judy and I. Rushing towards her we both tugged on her skirt and hollered "Go to the park and play games." We were growing up fast - outdoors no longer meant just the garden, it meant exploration and maybe a chance to investigate some wild-life. "That's what I thought," she said as she crouched down to our level. Turning her head to each of us she said "And who wants to help me push Stephen in his pushchair?" "Me, me, me," we both shouted. Our local park was only 10 minutes-walk away. Over time we called it 'the wreck', but I don't remember why. The wreck was a square green space with a few swings and a slide, and just beside it was a cinder running track. In the summer the grass was thick and luxuriant. In the winter much of the brownish black landscape was pitted with water-filled holes. The park was bordered by black prickly bushes and a road on one side, on the other side were more bushes hiding a housing estate, a field, and at the far end woodland. Just beyond the swings someone had tied a rope to one of the trees and fixed a tyre to it. The forlorn black tyre dangled some six feet above the ground; Dad stood under it one day – there was inches of space between his head and the threadbare tyre. We never saw anyone using it. The tyre would just merge into the landscape and remain forgotten about, but sometimes, to my excitement, it would blow round and round in the wind like a fairground ride. Occasionally we'd all venture into the blackness of the woodland; always with Dad or Mum. One day I was looking at the green tangled undergrowth and saw blobs of colour. "What a pretty plant - purple petals and just look at those shiny round berries.

Judy standing on tree-stump surrounded by Susan, Stephen & Dad.

Can I take some home Mum?" I pleaded. She caught my hand before I reached out to the black berries, "No, no, that's a Deadly Nightshade, it does look pretty but it's poisonous. Remember children – don't ever eat any wild berries unless Dad or I say so." I carried on searching, and found some yellow thistles. Looking up at Mum I waited for her answer. She smiled, nodded her head, and I plucked a few from the ground; my hands spattered with a milky substance oozing from the stems.

Outings to a park, or anywhere in the Surrey countryside soon became an integral part of our childhood. At weekends, when Dad was not working, we'd often take a bus, he said it was a mystery bus-tour, which brought us far away from the town. Mum and Dad carried the picnic hamper and rugs, and then our coats as the warm mid-morning sunshine melted the overnight mist. From the bus stop we all trudged into the dense woodland. Half an hour later the cool breezes under the tall trees ceased and a soft grassy area emerged – bathed in contrasting warm sunshine. "Can we stop now Dad, I'm hungry," I said. "Yes," he replied, "Lunchtime children." The hamper was opened, Mum passed round the Tupperware plates and mugs. Then the sandwiches, and as usual we three little ones fought over who got what filling in their white sandwiches. Mum poured fruit squash into our mugs and then handed out icing covered cakes - these were soon devoured as we hunched over our plates inspecting and eating every last scrap. We hadn't noticed that Dad had crept away. "Mum, have you got any chocolate," cried Judy, as she rustled her hands through the remnants in the picnic hamper. "Yes, but you've got to find it," she said – grinning and moving her head and arms from side to side. She pointed to all the bushes behind us. "Look there and there." Before she had finished her sentence, all three of us had thrown down our plates and had run to the bushes.

Picnic-time in the countryside.

Our little hands tore at foliage, branches, leaves and the tall grasses. We did the job of an efficient lawnmower, and soon all the chocolate bars were recovered from the now flattened shrubland around our picnic blanket. Mum took out a wet flannel from the hamper, and mopped our faces to remove the brown smears around our lips. Laughing, she said, "Glad to see you enjoyed your treats."

* * * * *

A sea of blue everywhere. I scanned the woodland in front of me – my darting eyes mesmerized by the bright blue shapes on the ground swaying softly in the breeze. Every now and then the Spring sunlight would filter through the trees and shimmer on the bright blue colours. "Mum, mum, it's beautiful," I cried. We'd arrived at what was to become one of our favourite haunts – a Sunday bus trip to the countryside south of the villages of Bletchingley and Godstone. Traipsing up the narrow lane from the bus stop we were met by this magical scene. We'd all seen bluebells before, but not on this scale. The blue haze seemed to go on forever and ever. Dashing through the delicate blue plants Judy and Stephen seemed to be just as intoxicated as I was. Judy twirled and skipped, calling out to both parents, "Mum, Dad, can we pick some and take them home?" "Can we?" I asked too. Dad held up the picnic hamper and said, "When you've eaten your sandwiches, then we can use the wet cloths to wrap the bunches in." The sandwiches and scotch eggs were soon devoured. "Don't forget your homemade lemonade," cried Mum as her three children ran towards the bluebells, not hearing or caring about what she had said. Soon, all three of us had gathered an armful each of the fragile rubbery stems. Mum wrapped up the delicate bundles for us to take home while Dad packed up the hamper.

Bluebells forever.

We children never forgot our trip to Tilburstow Hill and it became a regular yearly treat for us all.

* * * * *

"The old car is still there, look Dad," I shouted as I slowed to a halt. I'd run in front of the others, hoping to see the old car. We were on our usual weekend walk, this time to Gatton Park – only a few minutes from our house. Right at the beginning of Rocky Lane, on each side of the road, the drooping tree branches above almost touched each other as they nearly met in the middle. On the right-side in amongst the tangle of trees and bushes was an old gatehouse – long since fallen into disrepair. Beyond the stone house the vegetation was overgrown and neglected. Just visible through this jungle of greenery was the rusty skeleton of a car. We all peered through the mess of foliage to see the old car. Dad had previously told us the car seemed really old – maybe from the 1920s or 1930s. "Can we get nearer", one of us children said. "Well", said Dad, grinning at us all, "If you don't mind the spiders and other insects….". He began to hold back some of the branches – all entwined and twisted with endless strands of vegetation. He leaned hard against one of the strongest tangles; one by one we heard snapping and cracking as the branches broke and collapsed to leave a tunnel through the wispy greenery.

Sunlight flooded through the leaves providing a natural spotlight on the car. "Not a Rolls Royce," commented Dad, "Although, in its day, a fine specimen." I ran my fingers along the bare window frames, flakes of disintegrating brown metal fell to the ground. I looked at my fingers and then wiped the brown grit on my shorts. The rusty wreck seemed to command an air of dignity; not yet part of the surrounding flora, although the solid rusty metal was beginning to echo the colour of the Autumn leaves around it. I brushed away the ants that were crawling up my leg, and stamped on the dusty earth. “Why’s it been left here,” I said, my eyes warily looking down at my legs. “I don’t know,” replied Dad, “Maybe when the owners of the house moved out, they just left it behind.” We never did find out, and sometime in the next year the rusty car vanished.

* * * * *

“Can we go, please,” I said as I stamped my feet noisily on the lino. Judy joined in, both hands held tightly to Mums apron, nearly pulling it off her, “Oh please can we go, I’ll carry the baskets.” Stephen toddled into the kitchen, wide eyed and looked at the scene in front of him in slight bewilderment. Mum sighed, “Oh alright, but not till Dad gets home.” Before long we all trotted down the alleyway, Judy stomping out in front, swinging two brown wicker baskets in circles the air. Toddler Stephen was pushed along in his pushchair by Mum – he was oblivious to what or where we were going. We all crossed the road to where the almost vertical railway embankment met the pavement; several yards above, a train passed deafeningly along the track. In amongst the wild straggly bushes were hundreds and hundreds of berries – mostly black, some white, red or purple. Each fruit was made up of a cluster of tiny globules – packed with sugary moisture I soon discovered. The blackberry picking season had arrived. Our thoughts were of Mums crumbles oozing with blackberries, pies leaking red-hot blackberry juice, pavlovas dripping with squashed blackberries; heaven.

Both baskets were soon filled by four eager pairs of hands. In my excitement to pick the fruits, I'd punctured some of the delicate berries and accidently smeared my hands, forehead and skirt leaving deep red stains. I turned to face Mum, staring up at her eyes, a mischievous smile radiating across my face. "Susan", she yelled. She turned to face Judy, who also had noticeable red stains on her hands and clothing. "I told you two not to get in a mess – Andrew, look what they've done," she cried. Dad just shrugged his shoulders saying, "Time to go home now, and early bath-time I think." He winked at Judy and I and smiled.

* * * * *

Warm sunlight was banishing the cold frosty December morning to a memory. Little wellington boots were pulled out of a cupboard and pushed onto our waiting woolly socks and fidgeting toes. Coats, scarves and mittens were donned. We three little ones ran to the front door. Moments later Dad opened the door and we all sprinted out. Snow hadn't arrived yet, although in the coming days a soft white blanket would cover much of the land. White trails hovered in the air as us children chatted – all eager to outdo each-others mouthed trace marks. Stephen clung on tightly to Mums hand as we strode along the pavements. Dad carried the trug and secateurs. We were all on a mission - before every Christmas we would all go to the hedgerows in Rocky Lane.

Just the other side of the crumbling wall separating the main road from Gatton Park was a sanctuary of seasonal vegetation; holly, ivy and mistletoe in abundance. We three clambered over the knotted undergrowth. "Over here Dad", said Judy, pointing up to sprigs of sharp holly leaves. "And there are lots of red berries," she shrieked.

"And here too," cried Stephen as he peered up at one of the gnarled trees; he jumped up and down and waved both of his arms in the air in excitement. A few minutes later Dad had a trug full of carefully cut branches of holly and ivy. "Who can find some mistletoe," said Mum as she looked from one tree to another, adding, "Children, look out for the white berries." All our little eyes scanned the lower branches of the trees. Moments later Judy called out from behind a big, mature tree, "I've found some, here, here Dad," she screamed in anticipation; she ran to him, pulling at his clothes so he'd follow her. With the trug now overflowing, we all helped out by carrying a few stems of our scavenged plunder. Once home, steam rose from our mugs - hot cocoa soon thawed our cold bodies.

* * * * *

The sounds of giggling, laughter and more giggling followed by the sound of soft thuds. Mum looked over her shoulder, down the sandy slope towards where her children had been climbing up the bracken covered terrain. In amongst the large fern leaves she saw an arm appear, then part of a child's body as Judy emerged, heaving herself upright. More giggles, as Stephen stood up, shaking bits of brown bracken from his clothes. I continued sitting in my bracken nest. All around me were huge fern leaves, some up to two feet high; neither I nor my sister and brother had seen anything like it. I rolled over to crush moss green fern leaves and immediately the bracken I had been sitting on bounced back to its wavy vertical norm. Leaning on my elbow I pulled a fern leaf towards me and noticed how delicate it looked, yet it was so strong and springy; as I let go it bounced back to join its neighbour. I stood up, looked across at the heath – open, grassy, some undulating sand patches, a few trees with gorse outcrops here and there dotted with purple heather.

In the distance I could just about hear the slow hum of traffic on the main road and nearby the sound of birds chattering. “Susan, stop day-dreaming and follow us”, shouted Mum. Jolted back to reality I fought my way through the feisty bracken, re-joined the sandy track and trudged upwards.

We’d recently moved to Reigate from Redhill – Reigate Heath had become our new playground. On the way to this hillock, we’d walk across the golf course. No-one was playing that day. Approaching one of the sand-filled bunkers, Stephen peered over the edge of the grass tufts and then lay down. “It’s a sand-pit”, he cried, disappearing headlong into the spongy sand. We made our way across the heath discovering more bunkers; some round, some deep, some jagged in shape. And all filled with millions of creamy coloured grains - the perfect landing for our small feet as we jumped into each sunken pit, sand grains flying in every direction as we hit the ground.

“Nearly there,” puffed Mum, stopping to catch her breath. The hillock was steeper than she realised. We ran ahead, hopping and skipping. “Mum, Mum, can we go in the windmill,” we three said almost at the same time. “Please, please,” Judy cried as she hovered by the door to the windmill. “Let’s see what the notice says first,” Mum said. Judy shuffled to one side of the door. A moment later Mum lifted the iron door latch, pulled the heavy wooden door towards her, and us three bolted through the opening. “Calm down,” she whispered, “I told you that it’s a church. Behave yourselves.” We children gazed at the solemn interior and quickly felt the coolness of the air. Mum sat on one of the wooden chairs in the back row, soon to be joined by Judy and Stephen. I wandered around the tiny space looking at all the religious paraphernalia. I shivered – looked at the goose-bumps on my arm, saying, “Can we go back in the sunshine now.” All four of us ran through the open door. Laughing, I said, “Let’s pick some ferns and take them home.” Judy and Stephen ran down to the bracken shrieking, “Yeesssssss.”

* * * * *

10 Unlikely Toys

Lying in the cockpit we prepared to re-enter Earth's atmosphere. Judy, my co-pilot, manoeuvred our space car into position. "Hold on tight, here goes," she said. Our eyes were closed, both our heads horizontal and limbs relaxed – I could feel the cold air above my nose as I wafted around in the all-engulfing blackness. "Let's fly over Australia," Judy drawled. "Ah, um, yes," I replied. Sleep was overwhelming us both, but we pushed on. Pressing the button to my left, "Going down," I said - the space car zoomed down through the pure white clouds into the bright blue of our world. "Pull up, pull up," she cried, "We'll hit the ground." My sleepy arms reacted, fingers stabbing at several buttons on my control panel. Our space car corrected itself and hovered. "Seems like we are above a vast sandy desert; nothing but yellow mounds.... Stretching forever and ever" I commented. "This is boring," exclaimed Judy, "Why don't we fly somewhere else instead.... Somewhere with hills, or mountains? Yeah, lets fly to Switzerland." Mesmerized, I thought of the wind whooshing around all those snowy white peaks as they emerged from the cotton wool clouds. And the pure white snow lit up by the rays of the sun – glittering like jewels plastered across the jagged rock. A sudden noise roused us to alert status. "Shh," I whispered, "The aliens are coming."

The landing floor creaked as feet padded softly along its length. The bathroom door squeaked open, click went the electric light switch, then the door was carefully pulled into its frame. "That's ruined everything. Now I'm wide awake," I said. Both of us sat bolt upright, tossing our blankets from our bodies. Our imaginary control panels evaporated into pillows.

Turning, I threw my pillow behind me against the bedstead. Air exploded as my head crashed on the pillowcase. Dad or Mum had interrupted our game. Some nights, when we couldn't sleep, we'd play sleeping cars. We'd both place our pillows adjacent to our stretched-out arms; they became a control panel, shiny red buttons everywhere. Each bed could now fly. We would zoom around high up in the skies until our minds became intoxicated with sleep.

* * * * *

In amongst the wispy branches of the willow tree our den was created. The outside world was shut out. Now and then we'd hear the sound of a passing car from within the den, the noisy metal clutch grating as the car slowed at the junction to our road. Westway Gardens was circular, and at the beginning of the loop was a green - opposite our house. A perfect play area for us children. Just before the house builders departed, they left a few tufts of grass and a stumpy sapling in the middle of this area. Over time the green patch flourished and the stump grew into a shower of leaves and branches that over-flowed onto the luscious blades of grass.

As we stood inside this tree-cave the outside sunlight filtered through the feather-like leaves. And when the wind blew, as often it did in that exposed vicinity, the smaller willow branches swayed like an octopus. We'd left Stephen in his playpen in the garden; we knew he could amuse himself for hours by rolling his coloured bricks around his mat. So, we crept out of the back garden unnoticed and scuttled to the cover of our den. "Wonder if Mum knows where we are," we'd say to each other. Smirking and giggling I'd run my hands through the thin trailing branches. "Look, a ladybird," I'd say, as I pulled a few of the wispy leaves towards Judy. Her eyes loomed towards the creature. "Only two spots," she said, "I'll see if I can find one with more spots." Our hands were gently rustling through the leaves as we bobbed up and down looking for another ladybird. In the silent air we suddenly heard Mum calling to us. I parted the leaves, just enough for one eye to focus on the aproned figure of Mum standing in our front garden. Hands on her hips, she was turning her head to look left and right. "Susan, Judy," she called again. We both held our hands over our mouths to stop the noises coming from between our lips. "It's no good," I blurted out and we both shrieked with laughter. Moments later two arms and then her jazzy apron appeared through the leaves, she pushed her body into the den, "Ah, there you are," she said "Your tea is ready." Plodding across the green to our house I was almost annoyed that she wasn't angry with us.

* * * * *

Mum had a part-time job on the nearby industrial estate, as well as being an Avon lady, a Tupperware dealer and numerous other things. One day she bought home reels and reels of discarded tape for us and plonked the box on the lounge floor. We children peered into the open cardboard box; my nose was almost touching the tip of the dusty box. The pungent smell was overpowering - our heads reeled back, momentarily. The Bayko housebuilding set we had been playing with in the lounge was now abandoned – bricks, window panes, a roof and a door lay scattered on the carpet and forgotten by us. One by one we dipped our hands into the tall box to grab a reel. Holding the glossy tape with one hand I held it up to the light to watch it glisten. With my other hand I rolled and pulled it till the tape squeaked. Soon the air was filled with squeaks and laughter. Giggling, we three youngsters twisted and turned our bodies as we wrapped the brown tape around our clothes. The chemical smell was intense – a very strong, waxy nail polish odour. And the more tape we unravelled, the more appealing the acrid smell became. We entwined the open reels of endless squeaky tape around anything else within our sight; chairs, the coffee table legs, a window handle, the upright lamp, even the kitchen door handle.

An hour later Mum appeared from the kitchen, her eyes immediately fixed on the brown tape tied around the kitchen door handle. Looking at each of us in succession, her hands on her hips, head slowly shaking from side to side and mouth open. Our little bodies were writhing around and tangled up with shiny tape. And this spaghetti-like tape was also tied around much of the furniture in the lounge. Mums open mouth closed. A second later she grinned so much, I think she almost laughed. "Come on you three," she said," Time to clear up – it's tea time." She bent down to our level, sat down and began to untangle us from the ribbons of tape. "Tomorrow," she grinned, "It's back to your housebuilding set."

* * * * *

"Look at me," I cried as I turned around to look down from my new height across the garden towards Stephen. His little body was sitting on the grass playing with his toys, oblivious to the commotion happening just a few yards from him. When I shouted again, he looked up and saw Judy and I standing on the wooden rungs of a pyramid shape waving at him. "Look, look – see what Dad has made us," I said. Judy was giggling as Mum appeared from the house.

Susan & Judy standing on playpen.

She looked at Stephen who had toddled across the springy grass to see the new toy. Mum grabbed his arm and tugged him backwards, just before he too tried to climb the new toy. He tried to pull away from Mum – twisting his dungarees one way and then the other way. Squirming, he lifted one of his short legs towards the first rung moaning, “I want to go on it too!” Mum grabbed him again, and crouching down to his height she said softly, “I’ll help you up in a minute, wait till your sisters have climbed down.” Many of our toys and baby stuff had been handed down to each child and sometimes even lent to us by Mums cousins. One such piece of equipment had done the rounds, and our Dad, adapt at converting and making things, had turned our old playpen into a climbing frame.

* * * * *

Every summer we all stayed with Granny and Grandpa for a couple of weeks; they had retired to Lancing, a small coastal town to the west of Brighton. The seashore became our playground. At high-tide, between each of the old wooden breakwaters that disappeared into the sea, the beach was stuffed full of pebbles and shingle. Some summers we could see and smell the obnoxious great mounds of rotting seaweed too; black, slimy and sticky. As the sea retreated into the ocean, brown muddy sand was revealed. The sun’s rays soon dried the sand into a creamy yellow colour – building sandcastles naturally became one of our sea-side passions. We three children would trudge down to the seashore through the shingle, often nearly knee deep in the sinking stones, to reach the firm carpet of sand. Sometimes, we’d stop beforehand at the Mermaid café to buy brightly coloured paper flags to stick into our sandcastles.

When Judy and I tired of building sandcastles, Mum or maybe Dad suggested building sand-boats instead. Using our spades, we'd trace out a bath size boat shape in the sand - the front pointed end of the boat nearest the sea. Furious digging of sand, constant refilling of our buckets produced a wall for hull of each boat. In the middle of our 'boat' we'd construct a solid shape topped with bucket sized turrets. And this sandcastle-like shape was adorned with as many flags as we could cram onto the towers. And all the sand-building, be it a castle or boat, was always done with Dads enthusiastic help.

"Don't you think this is the best ever boat," I gestured to Dad. "No, it's not," retorted Judy, her voice and head raised "Mine is." We both sat inside our boats, Dad standing between us, barefoot on the beach as the sea lapped around his shins. The tide had turned and the seawater was creeping over the pointed bow of my boat. I jumped out of the boat and filled my bucket with wet sand. Splashing through the deepening swirling water I waded to the front of my boat; adding the sand to the collapsing wall. Judy's boat was slightly behind mine, and still in pristine condition. "Well, I think it's a draw," smiled Dad – forever one to try and keep the peace between us children. "But it can't be," shouted Judy, now standing upright and waving her hands wildly in the air. She pointed with one of her tanned arms to the turrets in her boat and stamped her feet, "Mine has more flags, so it's more important.....so I've won." And most beach trips ended with Judy or I yelling to anyone who happened to be on the beach that "My boat is better than yours," or, "I've won, I'm the winner."

Back home at Granny and Grandpa's bungalow, stopping at the front door, we'd take off our sandals, tip them upside down and watch the sand and small pebbles trickle to the ground. Our tired little bodies were smeared with dried sand; our beach clothes were peppered with the tiny grains. We were de-sanded in the bath – the murky bathwater, once drained, left a grimy ring of brown scum half way up the inside of the tub. Leaping into clean clothes we raced each other to the garden. "I'm getting in today," I would shout as I jumped into the box. Judy helped Stephen climb in too. The box was actually a metal wheelbarrow, but shaped like a square box, with two black wheels either side and a big red handle behind. Sometimes, we three would squeeze into the box – Judy or I having to stand, so Granny and Grandpa could push us around the garden.

* * * * *

We all loved looking at the riot of colour created by the vibrant flowers in the garden, and as we grew older, smelling the intoxicating fragrancies of different varieties of flowers. The sweet scent of Mums rose bushes were particularly overpowering. But a few rose stems in a vase could not fill a whole room with their scent, so one day Mum asked us to help her make rose water to leave in jars around the house. Judy and I scampered into the garden, with our tiny garden trugs, to brave the prickly rose bushes and find the perfect rose petals. Sniffing out the best smelling pink ones, yellow, white and of course red roses was easy for us girls, despite the elbow fights and scratched skin on our little bodies where the prickles had won. After Mum heard raised voices, for the umpteenth time, 'I've got more than you' she called us in to the kitchen with our treasured plunder. We ran back to our toy-room, the lean-to, to find some of our normal toys to squabble about.

Granny & Grandpa pushing us children round their garden.

An hour later a sweet smell wafted from the kitchen. Mum appeared saying, “Here is a jar of fresh rose water to keep in this room. Sniffing, she said, “Does smell like a beauty parlour,” a prolonged sniff, “for posh ladies.” She looked at our mystified faces and explained. “Oh Mum,” I cried, “Can we pretend to be in a beauty parlour?” Smiling, she disappeared into the kitchen and returned with a striped seersucker tablecloth and one of baby Stephens clean terry toweling nappies. “You'll also need some face cream – Susan, you can find some in the bathroom cabinet,” she said. I ran upstairs to the bathroom and rummaged through an assortment of bottles and jars. Vaseline, yes, that will do I thought. I didn't know what Vaseline was, but its creamy white texture seemed to be just right for a face massage.

In the lean-to Judy was sitting in the middle of the room with her protective cape, the tablecloth, wrapped around her body. Her little hands were jumping up and down beneath the tablecloth. “Come on,” she screamed, “I'm all ready.” Her hands and arms moving more and more as she eagerly awaited her face massage. I adjusted the white toweling that Mum had wrapped around Judy's head, the cotton nappy, pushing it back to reveal all of her forehead. Now,” I said with authority, “Close your eyes, head back, it's time for the treatment to begin,” and slapped on a dollop of cream to each of her cheeks. Round and round I swirled the cream on her soft skin. Every now and then her nose would jump up and she'd ask if I had nearly finished, until she let out a long sigh and said, “Am I beautiful yet?”

“Mum,” I called out, “What do you think? Mum, Mum....Muuum.” A minute later Mum appeared, wiping her hands on her apron. Looking at the open jar of Vaseline in my hand she laughed and said gently to me,

"Susan I meant the face cream, my Avon cream, not the Vaseline. I use that on Stephen's nappy r… well, it's really for medical use like putting on cuts on your skin." She pointed at the marks on my arm where the rose prickles had cut my skin. Judy was listening intently. "What have you put on my face?" she yelled and then stuck out her tongue at me. "Girls, girls, it's alright. Medical reasons mean it's just extra soft," she said softly while crouching down to Judy's eye level. "And Judy, you do look beautiful even with that silly nappy on your head. Susan, this was just a test run – next time use my Avon cream!"

* * * * *

11 Fun in the Garden

"Look at me, look at me," I cried as I stood up and looked at my brother and sister who were at the end of the garden. I was the tomboy of the family; my knees were frequently covered with plasters - now my bony knees and also my hands were smeared in dusty soil. And my summer clothes were dotted with brown smudges. I called out to them again, frantically waving a huge, rubber-like leaf across my grinning face. My little brother and sister stopped what they were doing, looked up and raced towards me. Giggling I said to them, "What do you think of my fan?" I held the pink stalk with my grubby fingers, the white roots dangling in the air. Fluttering the enormous fluted leaf in front of my face, to the left and the right, occasionally I turned my nose skywards. Not waiting for a reply, I stated in a snooty voice, "I'm the lay..dee of the maa..noor." All three of us erupted into chuckles of laughter. Both Judy and Stephen dived headlong into the rhubarb bushes; heads bobbing up now and then and arms scrabbling through the vegetation. "Let's go and show Mum," said Judy. We sneaked up to the kitchen door, Mums domain, and it overlooked our back garden. Judy and Stephen stood behind me clutching pink rhubarb stalks in their fists, and hiding their faces behind their rubber-like fans. Our chortling subsided. I burst out, voice faltering, "Look Mum, what do you think of our fans?" Mum was standing at the kitchen sink. Turning, she saw her three small children hiding behind gigantic rhubarb leaves, softly sniggering. After a very long pause, no-one moved or said anything, except for the birds in the treetops she simply said, "I see you've picked the rhubarb for our pudding tonight." Wiping her hands dry on a towel she walked to the door, "Come on," she said, "I'll show you how it's done properly."

The kitchen was alive with the shrill sound of our voices. “I want this one,” I said, throwing down a discarded packet of seeds in front of my sister. “And I want pink flowers,” interrupted Judy. “Children, children, stop squabbling,” said Dad. “You’ve all had the same vegetable seed packets.” Dad’s high-pitched voice calmed, and he pointed to the remaining packets. “Just choose one variety each from the flowers,” he said with a heavy sigh. I held the glossy packet in my hands; a picture of pretty blue flowers appeared on the front. Magnificent Blooms I thought – I was sure the seeds would magically grow like those on the packet. Stephen and Judy made their choices, attracted also by the bright colours on the seed packets. We trooped into the garden clutching our seed packets like they were treasure. Mum and Dad had prepared three distinct rows for us; our own patch of soil and marked each row with a separate large stone with Su, J and St painted on it.

“Now, put your packets down by your stone. No, not there Stephen,” said Dad, as Mum grabbed the toddler by the straps on his dungarees. She steered him by his straps towards a garden bench, lifting his chubby body onto the seat. Immediately he slid down onto the grass and ran towards the rows of churned soil. This time, Mum put his tiny wheelbarrow beside him and handed him a small trowel; he played happily digging channels and craters in his row, oblivious to the activity that was going on around him. Following Dads instructions, Judy and I planted a few rows of carrot seeds. At seven years old I didn’t really understand the growing process.

Stephen busy gardening.

The little dried seeds in the packet didn't look anything like the juicy orange specimens on the glossy packet cover. I just did what Mum and Dad told us to do; carefully dragging a trowel along part of the patch to form a channel where we sprinkled a line of seeds and then patted the soil over our treasure. We did the same with the potato and lettuce seeds. Next came the watering cans. "Please Dad, can I fill it up first," I cried. But Judy had barged in before me and stood guard by the outside water tap – her eyes huge and daring anyone to come near her. As water spewed from the tap into her can she started flicking water at me. "I got here first, go away," she shouted. "Calm down, calm down – Judy, behave yourself," bellowed Dad. I turned from Dad's view and stuck my tongue out at Judy and then gave her a sneering smile. She waddled towards her vegetable patch, both hands prised around the handle of the metal can. Her little legs swayed from side to side – water splashed out from the top of the watering can soaking the front of her cotton dress. But she didn't seem to care. Turning her back on us she balanced the can on the edge of her patch, tipping the watering can slowly until the clear liquid dribbled from the spout onto the soil.

Whistling softy to myself I walked back to the vegetable patches holding my half-filled watering can. I looked down, beside the soil was a pile of bamboo canes, a ball of string and a pair of shears. I knelt on the grass and ran my fingers along the shiny brown canes. "What's that for Dad?" I asked. At that moment Mum came out of the garage carrying a tray of small black pots – a spindly green seedling in every pot. He pointed at the tray, "They're baby runner beans plants. We're going to make a frame for them to grow on – just like a long wigwam," he replied.

Susan & Judy - fascinated by watering cans!

My face must have lit up. "Ooo, can I help Mum, Dad?" I said, looking in wide- eyed wonder at both my parents. Before long Dad had organised us all into a gardening assembly line; I handed Dad the bamboo canes, he plunged them into the ground at regular intervals. Two canes would meet and crossed over about one foot from the top – the joint had to be secured with string. I wanted to do this, but even standing on tip-toes with arms stretched above me I couldn't reach the juncture, so with a woeful face I handed Dad the string to tie the canes together. Mum and I planted the tiny seedlings – one beneath each cane, Judy watered all the plants. The assembly line moved to Judy's patch and then Stephens' patch. Earlier, Stephen had got tired of digging holes and was running tirelessly around the garden, especially with one of the empty watering cans.

During the next weeks and months Judy and I spent many mud-filled happy moments weeding and watering these rows. Almost daily we would peer in wonder through the tall bamboo canes watching for any sign of growth from the runner bean plants. Slowly but surely the plants rose in height and entwined around each cane. Their green, thick and floppy leaves and bright red flowers expanded outwards; soon all traces of bamboo disappeared beneath the green and red wigwam. Our parents judged when it was the right time for us to harvest the runner beans and when to pull up the fully formed potatoes and carrots from the soil. I would pull out the carrots by their long green bushy leaves; usually each carrot was so deeply coated with soil, the orange stem and curly white roots were not visible.

Susan - the champion veg grower!

One day, in my enthusiasm, I'd shut my eyes and shake the carrot so violently until all the particles of soil had settled on everything around me. One day, that included my Dad. "Sooosan," he would thunder, as I ran behind the green wigwam with my orange carrot.

* * * * *

"I've found one," I said, as I held up one of Dads old shirts from the tangle of clothes. Both my sister and brother shrieked in agreement. They both continued stuffing screwed up newspaper into each leg of a pair of trousers that Dad no longer used. "We need a pair of gloves for his hands," I commented, "And something for his head, oh, and a hat." Earlier that day Judy and I had been out in the town with Mum and we had seen a boy pushing a wheelbarrow carrying a straw dummy, and bellowing into the air 'Penny for the guy', 'Penny for the guy'. Of course, once Mum explained to us all about Guy-Fawkes we decided that we wanted to make our own guy. Mum helped us tie up the trouser legs and shirt arms so the pieces of newspaper wouldn't fall out.

Before the skies darkened Dad would prepare the bonfire in our garden and get everything ready for the yearly event. Every November 5th (that I could remember) we'd have a bonfire in our back garden, as did most other families. Mum ushered us children outside – jet black skies and a chilly wind did not deter us. Our warm coats, scarves and woolly mittened bodies gathered around the lit bonfire. Every now and then the wind changed direction and warm smoky air would waft around us. "Not too close to the bonfire and be very careful," said Dad. He stood upright saying, "Now who wants a sparkler to hold?" a resounding 'yes please Daddy' screamed his children. When it came to my turn, I impatiently grabbed the sparkler from his hand. "Ow, it hurts," I screamed as I dropped the sparkler on the ground; it carried on sparkling in the damp grass until Dad stamped on it. I held my hand up for Mum and Dad to see. Two of the fingers of my mitten were singed; and the woollen fibres had melted revealing tiny holes. Mum took off my mitten and held my hand towards the light of the fire, but there was no visible damage to my skin. "Susan, I told you to be careful," shouted Dad. "Fireworks can be very dangerous. Go and stand over there with your sister and brother." He disappeared to the other side of the bonfire. A moment later, he said, "Stand back, I'm lighting one of the rockets." Whizz, sizzling and whoosh." Part of the black sky over our house illuminated with a rainbow of colours. More rockets followed and finally our guy was thrown onto the bonfire amid cheers and laughter from us three children. The next week Mum had to buy me a pair of brand-new woollen mittens.

* * * * *

Soft rose scents wafted in the breeze from the many varieties of roses in the flower-beds. Flowers with different smells, colours and shapes – star-like, pearl, striped, fluted, wispy, dragon-like, spindly, mainly planted by Mum. Although I don't remember how she found time to plant them. Us children often had the job of watering the garden – in Mum and Dads speech they actually meant "Caaaaar…fully watering…. all the plants and not your clothes". Late afternoon we would stand barefoot on the concrete path. Our shrieks and yells usually outdoing the ferocity of the water as it erupted from the outside tap. Metal cans and buckets clashed; cascades of water spewed onto the concrete surface soaking our feet and sometimes saturating our clothes.

We'd dash hither and thither amongst the flower-beds. "Dagons, Dagons," cried Stephen as he teetered on the edge of the lawn holding his watering can in front of him at head height. With his arm extended, water trickled from the horizontal spout onto the swaying snapdragon petals in the flower-bed; deep pink, bright yellow, sky-blue and creamy white. Lowering his arm, the water gushed from the can to turn the dry dusty soil into a sea of dark brown mud. One weekend, when we had actually watered the plants and not our clothes, as a reward Dad finally gave in and let us try using his garden spade, fork and manual lawnmower. He left them on the lawn for us. Stephen picked up the handle of the spade and tried lifting it. Somehow, he managed to get it to his shoulder height - the 45-degree angled spade hovered in the air before crashing down solemnly on the lawn. Judy also found she was not tall enough to even reach the handle of the garden implements when they were upright. But I could reach the handle of the mower so I tried and tried to push the machine forwards using all my weight, but time and again nothing happened. Mum and Dad were watching our efforts. Smiling and then grinning broadly Dad just said, "Maybe next year children."

* * * * *

"Look, I've found a cricket ball," I shrieked. The sound of little feet ran towards me. "Where, where," echoed in the air. Metal watering cans clashed again as my brother and sister nearly pushed me headlong into the peony bushes. Struggling to regain my balance, I pointed at a red, shiny spherical object in the foliage. My brother and sisters four brown arms prodded through the greenery; Judy's head moved closer to the waxy form. Moments later she giggled, and stood upright and looked directly at my face – she was two years younger than me but by now almost the same height. "Huh, you idiot, that's a

Mum & children - the new gardeners.

flower," she sneered. I knelt on the grass, knees resting on my wet dress and looked again at the cricket ball. A petal was just visible on one side – I touched the delicate shape, then touched the waxy sphere. Feeling stupid, I said in a defensive manner, my voice squawking, "So, it's a flower, but I still think it looks like a cricket ball," I stood up and turned towards the house. I glanced down at the now muddy patches on the front of my dress. Breathing in deeply I stamped my feet on the lawn and returned to the tap.

* * * * *

The relentless summer rain was smearing down the window panes. The noise - ebbing and flowing, did not cease. That Sunday the sky had clouded over in the morning – it was now afternoon and the air outside was still dark grey and foreboding. The electric light in the living room was switched on. All thoughts of gardening outside had long been abandoned; but there were no tears, no tantrums, and no "Mum, when can we go outside?" by any of us children. We were entranced by the contents of an old box that Dad had brought down from the loft. Mum or Dad had kept the childhood toys in the large, musty box for years. According to Dad, the toys were from the 1930s, although neither parent remembered who had owned them. The noise of the rain continued, but for once all three children were silent, except for an occasional happy sigh and chink of metal.

Dad put down his newspaper and looked at his children's endeavours. "So, who has built the best garden," he said. I glanced at Judy and Stephen, "We haven't finished yet," I said. Both their bodies were bent over brightly painted lead flowers and pieces from a miniature gardening set, in studious concentration. both totally engrossed. Apart from the contents of the box, there were several other pieces – obviously bought to add to the kit. Judy was busy 'pegging' her lead flowers into the holes in the dark brown flower beds. In frustration she'd often pull them out, scrabble through a mini box of crudely shaped roses or brightly coloured hollyhocks, and then start all over again.

My garden, in comparison, was a bit more sophisticated. I'd first pulled out a greenhouse, but had thrust the model back in the box. Replacing it with a brown lattice pergola, and then a fountain and pieces of crazy paving. And, flower-bed templates – they were heavy, had holes punched in them with a uniform grass-green border painted on. The best bit – I'd discovered a model of a gardener pushing his wheelbarrow.

No preparation, no cleaning up, and no wet, muddy clothes, we children spent many happy hours with our faces pointing downwards on the carpet playing with these toys, even when it wasn't raining. Perhaps then Mum got time to plant the real flowers in our garden!

* * * * *

12 Sounds and Big Screen

The older we three children grew, the pull of the big screen and the wider world beckoned. Mum and Dad found out that our local cinema, Redhill Odeon, had a whole Saturday morning devoted to children's entertainment. Going to the pictures became the catchphrase for all children of our generation. From the moment we woke on a Saturday morning we would chant "We're going to the pictures", over and over, much to the annoyance of our parents!

To begin with, Judy and I went together. We were so excited to be going somewhere on our own and soon forgot our parents' farewells as they left us by the foot of the slope. This was our first foray into, what became the highlight of the week (going somewhere without our parents and also topping school, Sunday school and even Brownies). We were kitted out in smart summer frocks – and Judy's hair was often adorned with a big pink bow on her head.

I remember the first time I saw the cinema I thought the building was so grand. It towered above the roadway in front and to the elevated railway to the side of the building. The forecourt sloped upwards, at the top of this, so I thought, hill was a massive flight of steps.... "Up, up, up..., to the heavens." I'd sing to myself. Not put off by this at all, our little legs would spring up the oh so steep steps to the entrance to the cinema. We couldn't wait to get in. Our excitement, was tempered only by negotiating the crowds of other little, squirming bodies who were also equally determined to get up the steps and into the cinema foyer. The noise was deafening. Every child, it seemed to us, was talking and yelling at the same time. Some managed to make their way to counters selling popcorn, chocolate or other goodies. Gripping Judy's hand tightly, along with our precious tickets, we found our way through the crowds of heaving bodies and made our way into the massive semi-darkened auditorium to find our seats.

I found our row, pushed Judy in before me then slumped into my red velvet seat - this was real luxury as I felt the soft springy cushion beneath me. Glancing around the sea of children, some sat quietly waiting for the films to begin whilst others roamed around the aisles yelling and screaming. I looked at Judy and without saying a word we smiled smugly at each other and realised that the naughty children we could so painfully hear and sec hadn't listened to their parents parting words, "And mind you behave yourselves."

The lights dimmed and a huge cheer swiftly followed. We were treated to cartoons involving the favourite characters of the day: Mickey Mouse, Tom and Jerry, Bugs Bunny, Popeye and so many more. My favourite cartoon character was Popeye; a one-eyed spinach eating sailor who became super strong each time he ate spinach. Although, spinach didn't do the same for me – I hated the stuff along with all the other weird things my Mum used to cook, like bubble and squeak – fried mashed potato and cabbage. Uck.

And there were the Westerns. Loads of Cowboy and Indian films which the boys loved as they were full of action and noise. "Bang, bang," echoed around the auditorium, and "Pap, pap, pap," went the cowboy's shotguns. Followed by the Red Indians violent "Swish, swish, swish" of their spears or bow and arrow. These films did though teach us, so we believed then, the difference between the goodies and the baddies. And cliff-hangers too – every week those legendary words “To be continued next week”, were accompanied by loud, dramatic music which left every child sitting on the edge of their seat in impatient anticipation wondering what may or may not happen next. I thought a week was a long time to wait. But in reality, when Saturday came round again, I had forgotten the storyline anyway.

When the lights came on at each interval, the ice-cream ladies appeared – these elegant usherettes walking casually up and down the aisles. The ladies would carry a tray, attached to a strap around their neck, loaded with small tubs of mouth-watering ice-creams and lollies for sale.

Mum had given us a few coins, in addition to our pocket money, as she knew we adored ice-creams. We’d join the unruly queue behind the lady. More often than not, we soon abandoned our good-mannered ways to join the crowd by pushing and shoving our way towards the tray of snacks. Looking up at the lady’s smiling face I held up my clenched fist and opened my fingers to reveal a shilling, then with my other hand I pointed to my chosen treat. Above the din and mayhem, I got my lolly or ice-cream. Moments later Judy would also emerge from the scrum – her tiny hands clutching a tub of ice-cream. Later on, when we met our parents outside the cinema, Mum was quick to ask: "Judy, where is your pretty pink bow?"

* * * * *

Cinema was to become an important part of our lives giving us a greater insight into the complex world of adults. By the time I was eight-years- old, in 1964, the entire country was gripped by Beatlemania, including us children, it didn't take much to persuade Mum to take us to see our first feature film – A Hard Day's Night, at the Majestic cinema in Reigate. "Mum, look at all those people," Judy shouted as we walked out of the carpark. But we had to walk away from the cinema to follow the heaving snake of bodies who were obviously queuing. "It goes round the corner," I said, not quite believing the sheer number of people in front of me. Moments later Mum said "And round again," as she pointed to the stragglers at the end of the queue. Pretty soon even more people joined the queue and like everyone else sandwiched into this line. And we couldn't hide the excitement and anticipation to see our idols on the big screen.

Unlike the Odean in Redhill, I thought, the Majestic was its poorer neighbour. The cinema was smaller and as you walked into the foyer a musty, almost mouldy smell greeted us. We certainly weren't the only people with twitching noses who made a beeline for the sickly smell of the sweets counter. Judy and I got to eat one of our favourite Cinema treats – ever lasting toffee strips. With one end of the toffee gripped firmly by our teeth we'd pull and pull till our arms were outstretched then slowly suck up the spaghetti-like stretched toffee. But often the toffee strands would bounce back and end up smeared across our faces, or on Mum as she tried desperately to make us behave. I can't say that I understood what was going on in the film, but I and everyone else seemed to love the music; at times the entire audience erupted into song which vaguely resembled the catchy songs on the screen.

A few months later we all went to see the film, Mary Poppins. The huge cinema screen was filled by the bright colours of animated creatures and humans – sometimes you couldn't tell the difference between what was real and what was a cartoon, and the song lyrics were so magical as they bounced around the auditorium and stayed in our minds for days, weeks and years. On the way home from the cinema both Judy and I hopped and skipped down the street singing some of the song lyrics "Supercalifragilisticexpialidosious." We didn't know what it meant and we didn't care; the whole world (that we knew of then) seemed such a happy and fun place to live in.

* * * * *

13 Ladybirds and Mo Lester

Ambling slowly along the footpath, I walked home from school. Mum and Judy were in front on me. “Susan, hurry up now, it’s nearly time for your appointment,” said Mum. She’d stopped, turned around and was looking directly at me while I continued dragging my feet along the dusty pavement. “Do I really have to go,” I almost whispered. My head was bowed, hands stuffed in the pockets of my school coat, legs no longer moving, except for one foot which repeatedly kicked a brick wall; scuffing my new school shoes. “Susan, stop doing that,” she shouted. Taking hold of my arm, she led me along the pavement saying in a calmer voice, “It’ll soon be over, and then we can get you some new scraps and maybe go to the Ladybird shop – how about that.” I raised my head, smiled and carried on walking along the residential street. We approached a dazzlingly white-bricked house; noticeably different from all the other houses in Nutfield Road – all, without exception, were tired looking brown-bricked boxes. And in the front garden of this gigantic sugar cube was a huge flagpole. At the top of a pole a Norwegian flag fluttered in the breeze, framed by the blue cloudless sky. Our dentist, Dr Morten, was Norwegian.

We were shown into the waiting room by a pretty receptionist. The piped soothing music had an instant effect on me; I no longer felt anxious. The whole environment added to the tranquillity I now felt, all four walls were covered in soft hessian wallpaper and the furniture was light-coloured with wooden flooring, Mum told me, it was Scandinavian in design – all very different to anything I had ever seen before. By contrast, our home was typical of most in the mid-sixties: floral green/grey wallpaper and all the furniture made from dark wood with military grey and burgundy fabrics and carpet. I settled down on one of the cream-coloured padded chairs and buried my feet in a fluffy white rug. Light streamed through the window and bounced off the light colours in the room. I was ten- years old. My last baby teeth, the four wisdom teeth at the back of my mouth, I was told, had to be removed. I stuck a finger in my mouth and prodded the offending objects; they weren't even wobbly. Would they be pulled out by pliers? I quickly buried that thought as Dr Morten appeared at the open door; suntanned and wearing a brilliant white tunic. "Hello Susan, time for your extractions," he said, glancing at my Mum and added, "Do you want your Mum to come with you into the treatment room too?" I looked at Judy who was sitting as close as she could to Mum – a slight worried look on her face. Standing, I shook my head, "No, Mum can stay with my sister," I replied in a near confident voice. "Excellent," he said with a grin.

I perched on the edge of the dentists' chair, my eyes scanning all the equipment around the chair. The young dental nurse said in a soothing voice, "Don't worry. Sit back in the chair and relax." She put a plastic sheet across my chest and wrapped it around my neck. Smiling at me, she momentarily held my hand. "Now Susan," said Dr Morten, "Remember what I told you last week about this procedure?" I nodded slowly, not wanting to dislodge the plastic sheet. "We are going to put you to sleep for a little while – using gas," he said "And when you wake up it will all be over." He reached across me to the instrument panel and unhooked a grey mask attached to a pipe. I closed my eyes, thought of scraps and new clothes from the Ladybird shop, as he put the rubber mask across my face. I sniffed the strong smell of rubber, then inhaled the anaesthetic. Some while later I woke to find the dental nurse mopping the blood that was oozing from my mouth. "All done," she said. She held a cup of liquid in her hand, "When you are ready, I'll help you to sit up and rinse your mouth with this." Gently, she pushed my back away from the chair. The cup loomed in front of my face. I grabbed it, took a large gulp and spat into the basin. Red liquid snaked around the gleaming white basin. I repeated this until the red turned to pink and then was almost clear. Coughing and sputtering as I sat up properly. I said in a muffled voice, "Can I go now please?"

Mum, Judy and Dr Morten walked into the room. "All went well," explained the dentist to Mum. "I've got some gauze pads for Susan. And some for you to take home," he said while turning to me. He crouched down to look me in the eyes. "You will get a lot of bleeding," he said. After a brief pause, he grinned. "No, I'm only joking, as usual," he laughed, "Just a bit of bleeding for a day or two, that's quite normal. Open wide," he said whilst pushing two of the pads to the back of my mouth to cover my toothless gums. We all traipsed along the brightly lit corridor and down onto the ornately tiled front step and walked towards the front gate. I looked up; the flag was still flapping in the wind and the sky was still bright blue. I kept my mouth closed, intent on biting into the gauze pads. Judy looked at me awkwardly. "Does it hurt," she whispered. Holding my jaw in my cupped hands, I nodded vigorously shaking my head up and down.

* * * * *

The scrap shop was only a short walk from the dentists. I think the shop was a newsagent as it sold a large variety of miscellaneous goods including newspapers. Judy and I made a beeline for the metal display stands jam-packed full of brightly coloured scraps. The scraps were sold in transparent cellophane bags, singularly or in groups, depending on the size of the image. The smell of cellophane was overpowering, but in a nice and cosy way. Both of us collected and swapped scraps with our schoolfriends by putting them in books and before taking them to school for our classmates to wrangle over. If I stood on tip-toes I could just about reach the higher racks. We quickly sorted through the bags – mesmerized by the colours, aroma and feel of the shiny cellophane.

Clutching our purchases, that Mum had paid for, we ran ahead to the Ladybird shop. "Susan, something special – that doesn't cost too much," said Mum, her voice echoing in the breeze. Running in I nearly tripped on the entrance step and made a beeline for the new-smelling dresses. Mum caught up with me as I was rummaging through this clothes rack. "Very pretty, but a bit too expensive," she said. My chin dropped and I sighed heavily. Noticing the disappointment clearly visible on my face she said, "But what about these?" I looked up to see her waving a pair of the most beautiful socks that I had ever seen. The short white socks had a two-inch wide band of pretty lace and brightly coloured beading on their cuffs. My face lit up, the smile right across my face just got bigger and bigger as I nodded my head up and down. "Peese Mmm," I said through tightened lips, not wanting to dislodge the gauze.

* * * * *

Back home I threw myself onto the sofa and curled up in a ball; holding my jaw and feeling sorry for myself. Mum sat down beside me, running her hands through my hair. "Would you like some ice-cream for tea?" she said softly, "I made some last night just for you." Immediately I sat up. My hands relaxed and wrapped around my boney knees, eyes shining, face beaming – no words were needed. I felt like a Princess as I sat on the sofa lapping up a bowl full of chocolate ice-cream. Looking beyond the kitchen door, I could see Judy and Stephen sitting at the table – every now and then casting envious eyes in my direction as they stabbed at their baked beans.

At bed-time Mum insisted that I lay a towel on my pillow. I stamped my feet on the bedroom carpet, saying through my clenched mouth, "But I don't need it." "Your mouth will definitely bleed while you're asleep," she remonstrated with me. "No, it won't, I'm alright now," I shouted. Five minutes later I gave in. The next morning, I lifted my head off the pillow and sat up, yawning, I turned to look at my pillow. The plain white towel was now spotted with pink shapes of varying sizes. I smashed the pillow with my fists. "Why are parents always right," I screamed at Judy.

* * * * *

A few months later, one weekend, Dad was sitting on an armchair reading the local paper while Mum busied herself in the kitchen and us children sat on the floor playing with our toys. "Dr Morten may be struck off," cried Dad holding out the newspaper at arms-length. Mum rushed in to read the article. We heard much 'tut-tutting' and 'really!' from both of them. Mum lifted up her head towards the ceiling, breathed in deeply, shook her head and said to the room, "Possible fr…aud. His bad rep…utation with fe…male patients – mo...lest…ed some of them." She shook her head, then took a sharp intake of breath and said, "I always thought there was something not quite right about him."

I looked up with a puzzled look on my face, “Mum, what’s struck off mean and who is Mo Lester?” I said. “Oh,” she said, “Just means he can’t be a dentist anymore.” I looked at Dad them Mum and said stubbornly, “And who is Mo Lester? Did Dr Morten and Mo tell too many jokes?” Mum and Dad looked at each other. “Good grief” sighed my father as he buried his head behind his newspaper. Mum, shifted from one foot to the other, realized that her husband wanted no further part in the conversation and eventually said, “Something like that darling.” She glanced again at Dads newspaper wall, then looked back at me. But, by then I was leaning over my toys actively playing with my Sindy doll – any thoughts of dentists far removed from my consciousness.

* * * * *

14 Gervase, and the Sand Quarry

One weekend, in Summer, we turned out of our alleyway into Frenches Road hopping and skipping along the pavement – happy and excited at the prospect of a new adventure. Judy and I were clad in shorts and the sun burned on our bare knees. "Children," hollered Dad, "Stop. I'll tell you when it is safe to cross the road." A moment later we both heard him shout 'Now'. On the opposite pavement, we then ran through the dark bricked railway arch, above our heads was the main London to Brighton railway line, so Dad had told us. I shivered in the cold, gloomy and dank atmosphere. Stephen, our four-month-old brother, had been left at home with Mum and Dad was in charge of us girls. Dad stopped momentarily to listen to the deafening rumble of a train thundering along above us. "The 10.29 from Redhill to Victoria," said Dad knowledgably. Dad was obsessed with trains and had been since he was a child. To us he seemed to know everything there was to know about the railway and trains and particularly steam engines - locomotives; he called them locos. To an extent his enthusiasm rubbed off on us too. But for me, the sand quarry he had told us about, just beyond the railway arch and loco yard, seemed far more exciting.

I ran towards the railway sidings in the yard. My little legs struggling to step over the many railway tracks and sleepers which were all covered with white mounds of sand glinting in the bright sunlight and resembling snow drifts. The quiet railway yard was sleepy, yet hiding so much weekday activity that we never saw. We looked at the abandoned locos and wagons, then Judy ran around a particular engine before looking at Dad with a quizzical look. Dad nodded, "Yes, I'll help you up." From one beaming face to another, "Well, go on," said Dad as he pointed towards the loco's footplate. He lifted Judy's 3-year-old body onto the steep steps and helped her into the cab. I followed, thankful of holding Dads outstretched arm as he pulled me into the cab. He turned to talk to Judy whilst I peered around the cab. Everything was black. I saw that Dad still had his back to me so I began touching dials, switches, cables and all the intricate bits of machinery that I could reach. Dad turned around and noticed my contorted face as I stared at the black marks on my fingers, and said, "That's the soot from the coal. The coal dust gets everywhere in a loco cab. But you shouldn't be touching things unless I say." I held my head high, glared at him and then wiped my hands clean on my clothes, banged my hands on my shorts in disgust and was immediately told off by my concerned yet angry Dad. "Oh Susan, your clean clothes – they are all dirty, oh what will your mother say," he said in despair. "I think we'll have a look around the yard instead." From then on Dad gripped our hands tightly that day as the three of us explored the yard and loco sheds.

A few months later all three of us were wandering around the yard separately looking at the locos. I stopped and said, "Dad, this one has a name, not a number like the other ones, and it looks friendly". Somebody had left their jacket and cap draped on the opening to the cab, and a China mug on the footplate. Judy shuffled towards me, we both looked up and peered at the mug and then the nameplate which was covered in blackened grime. I knew most letters of the alphabet, so, with Dads help I said out loud, "G, E, P. Is that right Dad?" Dad stood beside me, crouching down and pointing his finger at the third letter, he whispered, "it's an R." I started again, speaking to them both with more confidence,
"G, E, R, V, A, S – that's S for Susan," I said proudly. But the last letter defeated me.

The letter looked like an L I said. Dad was grinning broadly and said "I can see it is an E, and what does that spell – GER," he said very slowly and then continued with, "VA..." For a moment I was puzzled and then all of a sudden, I shrieked, "Daddy, Daddy, it's Gervase!" Judy and I both jumped up and down in excitement, of all the engines in the yard we had finally met Gervase.

Dad had told us about Gervase – over and over again. In fact, Dad knew everything about Gervase and I think he thought we ought to know too. But all I remembered from his many talks was that this special loco was named Gervase. "Do you remember," Dad said, "Gervase was built in 1900 and started working here in this very yard in 1949. And his wheel arrangement is 0-2-0." He held his arm out and pointed to a distant track which went uphill. Continuing he said, "Gervase was used to bank up the trains and loaded wagons of sand up that steep incline to the main line. And..." At this moment he turned to look at me. Horrified at seeing his young daughter standing on an upturned wooden crate with her tiny blackened fingers darting all over the loco's nameplate. He shouted at me, "Stop doing that Susan, I told you not to touch anything." "Well," I scowled, "I was only trying to rub the letters clean of all the sand and grease. It is an E." And then in defiance I rubbed my smeary fingers all over my clean white cotton shorts, jumped off the box and ran to the other side of the loco. Dad, clutching Judy's hand, found me, told me off and we all walked home together in silence. Nevertheless, we all came back, time and again to see Gervase.

* * * *

"Please, Dad, can we go to the sand quarry today? Please, can we?" I cried. We'd been coming to the

Holmethorpe Industrial site for a few years with Dad to see the locos – a weekend treat, so he said. Whilst Judy and I liked looking at all the battered and worn-out engines and wagons in the yard, we were far more interested in the huge sandpits beyond. To me they seemed like mountains of pure white sand and slightly mysterious. "Dad, Dad," I called out, "When can we walk through the sand quarry?" That Sunday Dad gave in and he had to leave his treasured locos behind. We started to walk across the sand mounds - random clumps of grass sprang upwards and swayed in the breeze. The sun shone and the light bounced off the mounds of sand making them appear a brilliant white. And the silence was dazzling too – a very strange feeling, not scary, just different: soundless except for the occasional noise from a bird roaming the blue sky above us. Beyond the pathway the fine grains of sand and grasses quivered rhythmically in the breeze. I veered off this lightly trodden pathway, and found that much of the sand was not as firm as the track, so I began sinking and having to pull each of my sandaled feet one at a time very slowly out of the ground before I lurched into my next step. Not a good idea I thought and I soon made my way back to the pathway and the security of Dad. The site was massive. We caught our first glimpse of the distant quarry works – strange grey steel buildings thrusting out of the mountainous sand hills. The sight of these grey shapes made me shiver. Suddenly my paradise of sand and swaying grasses was shattered and I felt nervous. Silence, the breeze had disappeared too and there were no signs of activity anywhere. I reached out for Dad's hand and realised that Judy was holding his other hand too with a frightened look on her face.

Here and there large deep blue pools of water punctuated the landscape. Looking around I saw there were rusty metal poles that had been pushed into the sand with red signs warning people not to go near the water. “Dad,” I said, “Why can’t we go near the water?” As ever Dad knew the answer. “Because it’s dangerous,” he said slowly. “You can easily slip on the steeply sloping sand and fall in. And the water is cold and the pools are very deep.” For once I listened to him. “Okay Dad,” I said as I reached out for his outstretched hand.

Beyond the pools of water huge swathes of long grasses began to dominate either side of the pathway. Judy and I ran towards the grasses. These massive clumps towered above us. Here and there as we pushed through the soft grasses butterflies appeared. Most were small and white. Then we saw a splash of red and black fluttering towards us, much larger than the white ones. “Daddy,” I cried out with excitement, my hand and arm pointing towards the butterfly, “What’s that?” The majestic goldy red butterfly had landed on top of one of the long grass blades – thankfully well out of my reach. Dad didn’t need to get close to the butterfly to know what it was. “It’s a Red Admiral, and I’ve even seen some in our garden on that big bush of buddleia.” I stood on tiptoe, so did Judy, both my arms now pointing to the red blob. “Can I touch it please?” I said. Grinning broadly, he shook his head saying “No, we don’t want to frighten the delicate little creature. When we are back home, we’ll hunt for one in the garden – but no touching, just looking,” he said sternly although he was grinning at the same time.

We continued along the track for a little while then headed back to the loco yard. Dad could see that his children were both tired – our little legs were barely moving. He picked up Judi, took a last look at Gervase, and said, “That’s enough excitement for one day – I think it's time to go home for a cup of tea and buns." Despite being worn out, we both squealed "Yes please Daddy."

A few years later when our brother Stephen was old enough, he joined us on our Sunday adventures. But he never got to see Gervase at the yard in Holmethorpe as Gervase went to a new home in the summer of 1962. At first, Stephen would just hold Dad's hand and we'd hear him mumble the occasional "Choo, Choo train," Dad continued his endless train-talk; wheel description and other (boring) complicated stuff which went on and on - so it seemed to Judy and I. Gradually Stephen would join Dad in these discussions until our Sunday adventures were dominated by a constant stream of a two-way train natter.

* * * * *

When I was 11 years-old we moved to our new house in Reigate. By then all our holidays and day trips out involved something to do with locos and railway stuff. When I was about 14, I remember that one day Dad drove us all through the countryside of Surrey to Kent and we ended up in a place called Tenterden. And at many stages of that journey, every time we motored over a railway bridge, Dad would whistle. Pretty soon, we children all joined in too, and the occupants of the little blue car gave a loud phweeeeee sound as we drove over a railway bridge. Mum had been in charge of reading Dad's notes as he'd meticulously plotted the route from maps. And it was no surprise to us girls as the car turned a corner in a tree-lined lane that we were met by a huge roadside sign revealing our destination - the Kent & East Sussex Railway.

As we drove into the car-park Dads face lit up and he impatiently rolled down the car window – the smell of the steam engines was overpowering. He took a deep breath and grinned even more. Mum, Judy and I were not at all interested in seeing the trains so we went to the café whilst Dad and Stephen charged off towards the platforms. And Stephen did get to see, and climb aboard, Gervase, as well as the other locos and to look at all the old-fashioned railway paraphernalia of a long-gone era. The drive home was dominated by male voices discussing in detail their magnificent day out. Mum drove us home. Judy and I, trapped inside the tiny Ford Anglia, tried not to listen to the endless train talk, and occasional loud phweeeeee, phweeeeee, phweeeeee sounds. Eventually we both fell asleep and not so much by the rhythmic motion of the car. Although, luckily for us all Mum didn't fall asleep!

* * * * *

Stephen aboard Gervase.